MODERN SUDANESE POETRY

African
POETRY
BOOK SERIES

Series editor: Kwame Dawes

MODERN SUDANESE POETRY

AN ANTHOLOGY

Translated and edited by Adil Babikir

Foreword by Matthew Shenoda, supervising editor

University of Nebraska Press / Lincoln

The African Poetry Book Series has been made
possible through the generosity of philanthropists
Laura and Robert F. X. Sillerman, whose
contributions have facilitated the establishment
and operation of the African Poetry Book Fund.

Library of Congress Cataloging-in-Publication Data
Names: Babikir, Adil, editor, translator. |
Shenoda, Matthew, writer of foreword.
Title: Modern Sudanese poetry: an anthology /
translated and edited by Adil Babikir; foreword
by Matthew Shenoda, supervising editor.
Other titles: African poetry book series.
Description: Lincoln: University of Nebraska
Press, 2019. | Series: African poetry book
series | Includes bibliographical references. |
In English; translated from the Arabic.
Identifiers: LCCN 2019001566
ISBN 9781496215635 (pbk.: alk. paper)
ISBN 9781496218216 (epub)
ISBN 9781496218223 (mobi)
ISBN 9781496218230 (pdf)
Subjects: LCSH: Arabic poetry—Sudan—
Translations into English. | Arabic poetry—20th
century—Translations into English.
Classification: LCC PJ8314.5.E5 M63 2019
| DDC 892.716—dc23 LC record available
at https://lccn.loc.gov/2019001566

Set in Garamond Premier by E. Cuddy.

CONTENTS

In this seminal collection of modern Sudanese poems, translator Adil Babikir has introduced English-language readers to a significant gathering of largely unknown works in English. Translated from Arabic, these poems capture the often tumultuous and complex histories and cultural intersections in Sudan's modern period. Anchored in the mid- to late twentieth century, these poems give significant insight into the rise of Sudanese nationalism and the period of independence. Beautifully contextualized in an introduction by Babikir, this anthology traces the internal cultural negotiations of the Afro-Arab and Jungle and Desert schools that have defined and shaped modern Sudanese identity and helped define the emergence of a new poetic school in Sudan. In poems often steeped in a lyrical ornateness and sensual engagement with language, we are reminded of the intersections of history, place, and culture throughout this collection.

Linguistic embellishments paint landscapes both internal and external, and the poems gathered here make space for an important articulation of Africa's expansive story through a country that sits at the border of myriad multiplicities. So often these poems navigate the complexities of nationhood, place, and identity, poems like those of Mohyiddin Faris, where he writes:

The peels of words sing out;
the sun confiscates them,
but they confiscate her golden howdah,
and braid her hair into a guillotine,

to shear off the necks of the old times,
and open up our locked doors.
   ("The Horse and the Wind")

But the poems gathered here are far from singularly political. With verse that engages the depths of love, longing, religion, and culture, there is a consistent sense of ripeness that carries throughout. Fresh in their belief that the communal heart is the core of the human experience, these poems often remind us of just how supple and fluid language can be. Muhammad el-Mahdi el-Majzoub shows us the intimacy of these communal moments in his poem "Wedding Parade" where he writes:

Tonight, mother of the bride, we brought you
our cream of the cream;
palm fronds in our hands,
a good omen for green times to come.
Virgins as soft as young plants,
nursed in the shades for blooming time.
Rapture flying out of the drums,
like flocks of birds taking to the sky,
as the wedding parade gaily slid along the Nile bank.
We would catch rare glimpses of unguarded beauty,
yet we never go beyond the limits.

Perhaps more than any other poetic tradition hailing from the African continent, the Sudanese poets gathered here grapple with an African/Arab confluence in ways that show a rich and layered entanglement that expands our sense of binary identities and helps create a more nuanced and textured sense of north and south. What's perhaps most engaging about these poems is that nothing is taken for granted; the expressive energy found in each of these poems engages a kind of reaching, a desire for a deeper sense of understanding one's self in the context of a specific moment and place. This is the hallmark of all great poetry, a mirror that does not simply reflect our own image back to us but rather allows us to see ourselves anew.

ACKNOWLEDGMENTS

This anthology cannot claim to be representative of all the poetry currents in Sudan. It is only meant to offer a glimpse of the poetry scene in post-independence Sudan, a scene about which little is known in the English-speaking world. I do hope this modest attempt encourages others to bring to light some of the hidden treasures of Sudanese poetry.

Many friends contributed to this work. I am particularly indebted to Lemya Shammat, who patiently reviewed a good part of the selected poems and contributed invaluable comments. In writing the introduction to this anthology, I benefited from her comprehensive review of Abdel Goddous al-Khatim's book *Reflections on Sudanese Culture*, 2012 (Abdel Karim Mirghani Cultural Centre). The introduction also benefited from invaluable notes shared by Aalim Abbas, and from Kamal Elgizouli's excellent paper "The Hole in the House Roof." I am thankful to Dr. Al Haj Salim Mustapha, who lent me some invaluable references and opened my eyes to many shortcomings. I am grateful to Osman al-Jaali, Samia Kergwel, Mustapha Adam, Ahmed al-Nimeiri, Bushra el-Fadil, Murtada al-Ghali, Abdel Mone'm Agab al-Faya, Abdel Azim Abdel Raheem, Hamza Babikir, and Nizar al-Imam—among others—for their encouraging words and insightful comments.

Najlaa Osman Eltom was a great help, not only for offering three of her poems for translation, but also for introducing me to the works of the young generation of poets who are making waves in Sudan's literary scene today. A very special thank-you goes to my daughter, Mayada, who, apart from making some subtle remarks that I found quite useful, rendered her own translation of a long poem by Rugaia Warrag.

Obtaining the publishing rights proved to be an uphill task that entailed marathon trips and exhaustive search. I am indebted to many friends who helped me out. I owe a huge debt of gratitude to Mohammed Ahmed Yahya, without whom I would not have been able to secure publishing rights for such an important poet as Abdel Raheem Abu Zikra. Sadly, however, my efforts to obtain permission for the late great poet Salah Ahmed Ibrahim have failed. The plan was to include four of his poems: "Death and Us," "In a Strange Land," "Think with Me Malwal," and "Maria." Those would have been great additions to this collection.

INTRODUCTION

Notes on Modern Sudanese Poetry

The Arabic poetry in Sudan has come a long way. In the past six decades, which is the focus of this anthology, poetry in that Afro-Arab country has seen significant development in both form and content. While the development in style almost echoed the same pattern seen in other Arab countries, thematic development showed some distinctive features.

Traditional poetry, based on metrical verse, was the dominant style until the first half of the twentieth century. Starting in the early 1950s, that dominance began to fade away gradually in the face of new rhythms based on *taf'ila* (the single foot) as the metrical unit, which gave poets the freedom to use multiple feet per line. The 1980s saw the birth of the free verse (prose verse), which continues to dominate the scene today.

In terms of themes, Sudan's poetry landscape reflected conflicting views on identity, from *purist* voices boasting direct descent from the Arabian Peninsula to others asserting African roots. El-Nur Osman Abbaker once pronounced:

I never left my father's home,
to live in a desert cave,
 ("Al-Manfaa wal Mamlakah" [The Exile and the Kingdom])

Indeed, the issue of identity has always been the subject of heated debate between poets and intellectuals. El-Nur stirred a big controversy when in 1967 he wrote an article with the provocative title of "Lastu Arabiyyan walakin" (I am not an Arab, but . . .): "Everything that is transcendental and deep is but a product of the jungle.... The main thread in our existence is not Oriental Sufism but rather the melodious motions of the jungle dances; the drums; the horn."

That article triggered a tirade by fellow poet Salah Ahmed Ibrahim. "No, Nur. Actually, we are the Arabs at their best, a combination of the best attributes of the Arabs: nobleness and generosity; and the best attributes of the Negros: rigor and ardor" (1967).

Both el-Nur and Salah, however, shared a strong commitment to synthesizing Arabism and Africanism into a hybrid identity. At the end of that same controversial article, el-Nur asserted, "There is no historical evidence to nullify the fact that the Arabs did enter this land of the Negros, who had discovered it before the emergence of Prophet Mohammad. Nor is there historical evidence to deny the role of the simple Islamic teachings, in their Sufi, ascetic, non-academic form, in enriching the transcendental thought and conscience in the land of the Negros. However, only through joint struggle and endeavors to stoke progressive revolutionary awareness can the crossbreed of the jungle and the desert yield a much higher return."

That call for "joint struggle" echoed a similar call by Salah, in an emphatic appeal to "his cousin" Malwal (south Sudan):

> Think with me, Malwal,
> what a glory we can build together
> on the Nile bank,
> if we both in good faith came together!
> Think with me, Malwal,
> before we are split apart
> in the name of a stupid feeling of dignity,
> or in the name of the Lord,
> when the enemies stoke memories of old grudges.
> So let us disclaim them all.
>   ("Fakkir Maie Malwal" [Think with Me, Malwal])

The call for Afro-Arabism found inspiration in the great poet Muhammad el-Mahdi el-Magzoub, who is widely regarded as the godfather of the Jungle and the Desert current. In the early 1950s, he had a confession to make:

My veins are endowed with stubbornness from the Negros
My verse is endowed with eloquence from the Arabs.

("Fajrun Kathoob" [False Dawn])

He also made a bold wish:

I wish I were among the Negros
My steps swaying to the rhythm of my rabab
Free to gulp marisa in pups
Gobbling freely, to no one's discontent.
Even falling on the street.
My eyes blurred by liquor,
lit up with outrageous rapture;
Unrestrained by ancestral nobility claims
of Qurayshis or Tamims.[1]

("Intilaq" [Freedom])

El-Magzoub's pronounced wish reflected frustration at the hegemony of traditional Arab culture. It was a reminder to intellectuals that they had African blood running in their veins. According to Abdel Goddous el-Khatim, el-Magzoub's emotional pieces about Africa were driven not by a search for political identity but rather by pure longing for the "innocence of early humanity" (2012). That early wake-up call inspired a group of young poets to probe a way out of the polarization between Arabism and Africanism. That gave birth to the Jungle and the Desert school. Mohammad el-Makki Ibrahim, one of the pioneers of that school, describes his "girlfriend" as *khilassiyah* (one of mixed racial descent) as "partly Negro, partly Arab, and for sure, some of my words before the Lord":

So blend me,
with the graves of tropical flowers,
with the tearful times,
and ages of slavery.

("A Drib of Your Nectar")

Mohammed el-Makki Ibrahim, who is featured in this collection with four poems, is widely regarded as one of the icons of modern Sudanese poetry. His first collection, *Ummati* (My Nation), came on the high tide of global socialism of the 1960s. Capturing that mood, the collection's underlining tone was outpouring and enthusiastic. This is particularly evident in his poems in praise of the October 1964 revolution in Sudan, which toppled a totalitarian military regime that jumped on power after only two years from independence.

> The land is singing your green name, O October
> The fields have burst into wheat, promise, and hopes
> and the land, its troves flung open, is chanting:
> With your name's blessing, the masses have made it to victory,
> the jail walls are down
> and the chains are bracelets dangling
> from a bride's wrist!
>   ("Songs for October: [2] The Green October")

In "Qitar al-Gharb" (The West Train), Mohammed el-Makki takes us on a ride across the country from al-Obayyid in the central west to the capital Khartoum. He draws cinematic images, full of motion. Look at this lively scene at the railway terminal:

> In my land, the people have a nice smell;
> Smiles, greetings, and emotional farewell,
> and the bitter feeling of parting.
> Here is a woman, sobbing
> and a man concealing his tears in the sleeves of his robe:
>   "Give my greeting to all. And don't forget to write to us."
> The west train jolts, glides languidly on the rails,
> chased by relatives breathlessly delivering last minute messages.
> Waving hands.
> Smoke.
> And ululations: There is a bridal couple on board.

In another shot:

In the valley of forbearance
everything here is dull and pale
Everything is the color of the grave
Forbearance. Forbearance. Forbearance.
Huts tilting but never fall down
Trees withering but never die
People have long life spans, like whales
They are alive only because a father went to bed with a mother
and she gave birth to an axe
to tear down the land's heart
and dig out its troves
to keep the stock market in business.

Afro-Arabism, to its proponents, is a conscious effort to recognize the African blood and study a long-neglected aspect of their heritage, the Negroid heritage. According to Abdullahi Ali Ibrahim, the call for retrieving the African blood was meant to scale down northern Sudan's sense of belonging to Arabism so as to bring Afro-Arabism into balance. "In this context came el-Nur Osman's proclamation 'I am not an Arab, but...' and Muhammad Abdul-Hai's dismissal of the claim of Arab descent as a shallow vanity."

In Abdul-Hai's long poem "Sinnar: A Homecoming," the following conversation takes place between the persona and the guards of Sinnar, capital of the Islamic state of Funj (1504–1821), the first Afro-Arab Islamic state in Sudan:

"Are you a Bedouin?"
"No...!"
"From the land of the Negros?"
"No...."
"I'm one of you. A lost wanderer,
Singing in one tongue praying in another,
Returning home from distant seas."

Salah Ahmed Ibrahim stands out as a cultivated intellectual who is highly acclaimed for his superb poetry. His first two collections, *Ghabat al-Ababnous* (The Ebony Forest) and *Ghadbat al-Hababa'y* (The Rage of the Hababay), are replete with references to Greek mythology, theology, and Arabic and African heritages. He was an outspoken opponent to all forms of suppression and lived up to his principles until the very last day of his life. In the early 1970s he resigned his diplomatic post as Sudan's ambassador to Algeria in protest against the execution of Communist Party leaders and took political asylum in Paris, where he led an austere life as freelance writer.

Salah's complex trajectory as a poet can be used as a mirror of major turbulences in his country and in Africa at large. From the very beginning, he presented himself as an outspoken campaigner against oppression and injustice. His political poems are biting and sarcastic, drawing on a solid knowledge of history and international affairs. His furious tirades against the colonial powers across Africa served as an eye-opener to the atrocities and conspiracies against the African people. His emphatic elegies for the great Congolese leader Patrice Lumumba decried the malpractices of the colonialists and exposed the role played by the then military rulers of Sudan in the conspiracy that led to Lumumba's liquidation. His collections are replete with elegies for friends, family, and scores of obscure people, like Mebior, a young man from South Sudan who died during demonstrations against the dictatorship of General Ibrahim Abboud, which culminated in the October 1964 Revolution:

Up there in the realm of light he passed away,
our friend, a chap from the south called Mebior.
In the morning he softly comes along like a morning breeze
lending joy and delight to every soul
with a shining smile
and teeth lined up like a gaggle of geese
on the serene waters of the River Jour.
   ("Mebior")

Salah's sympathy with the less privileged and downtrodden comes perfectly natural in its outpouring. "Fil Gurba" (In a Strange Land), an outcry against racial discrimination, eloquently depicts the bitter feelings of estrangement in exile.

> Have you ever tasted the humiliation of color?
> Seen people pointing at you, shouting:
> Black nigger! Black nigger!

In "Death and Us," a tribute to his family members whom death had snatched one after the other, Salah is extending an open invitation to death to feel free to come whenever "you craved for more."

> Hover over our quarters, O death.
> Line us up in the open.
> Handpick every noble, merry, and faithful,
> every forbearing and cheerful,
> openhearted, open-handed.
> When he warmly greets you at the door,
> with an inviting smile,
> and an immaculate heart—
> thrust your nails into his chest
> and snatch his soul.
> And please, O death,
> whenever you crave for more,
> do come along and be our guest,
> and see for yourself what a living legend we are,
> defeating extinction, outliving demise.

Besides Salah, scores of Sudanese poets—and fiction writers—were influenced by the strong waves of socialist realism in the 1950s and '60s. Those include Jayli Abdel Rahman, Taj el-Sir el-Hassan, and Mohiyiddin Faris. The three of them studied in Cairo and quickly made their way to the fore of the literary scene in Egypt. Their poems, which were published in Cairo's major literary magazines and newspapers of the time, mirrored the frustration and broken dreams of the poor and marginalized.

Cairo saw the rise of another Sudanese star: Mohammed el-Fayturi. Born in Sudan to an Egyptian mother and a Sudanese father of Libyan origin, el-Fayturi lived a good part of his early life in Egypt and became a prominent figure in the Egyptian literary scene. His enthusiastic poems reflected the high mood of nationalistic aspirations in the Arab world and Africa.

The influence of Russian poetry was particularly palpable in the poetry of Jayli and Taj who spent some time there. Jayli's poetry presented a new style of expression that was a direct reflection of his life experience as a nationalist struggler. He lived in extreme poverty, but he never lost his optimism, resolve, and commitment to his class. Life in Cairo's impoverished neighborhoods featured prominently in his poetry. In terms of style, Jayli and Taj were among the first in the Arab world—along with the prominent Egyptian poets Salah Abdul Sabur and Ahmed Abdul Mu'ti Hijazi—to adopt *taf'ila* (the single metrical foot), a major departure from the classical rhymed form. That new form was more in tune with the new ideas and concepts addressed in their poetry, which echoed the aspirations of the deprived population. Even a quick read through the titles of Jayli's poems will sufficiently tell how deep and genuine his commitment to that cause was. The list includes "Sorrows of a Nubian Village," "The City Streets," "Children of Zahrat al-Rabi'e Block," "Dawn at a Village," and "Migrating from Sai," among others.

"Hijra min Sai" (Migrating from Sai) is a retrospective of nine-year-old Jayli's journey to Egypt in the company of his mother to join a father who had left the village and settled in Cairo before the birth of his son. It contains a series of vivid images that combine to draw a movingly sad picture:

> The women piled up on the shore
> like heavy memories on the heart
> of a heartbroken poet.
> They kissed my mother's face
> and waved to the loaded boat.
> My uncle was wetting my tiny head,
> with incessant flow from his gaping, deep-set mouth.
> His coarse beard was pricking my cheek;
> his moustache flirting with my eyelids;

his tears flowing copiously down his cheeks.
"Son,
if you get there safely
and all went well,
tell your father to think of his brother,
to remember him, despite the distance."

Taj's poetry is full of nostalgia. His tone is revolutionary and outpouring.
He was a loud anti-colonial voice. His "Afro-Asian Song" celebrated the birth
of the Non-Aligned Movement in 1961 as a brilliant endeavor by Third World
countries to break away from the yoke of superpowers. That poem eloquently
captured the high mood that swept the Third World as leaders from Asia,
Africa, and Eastern Europe met in Bandung, Indonesia, to set a new course
for their independent states:

When I play our ancient songs, O my heart,
as dawn lands on my chest aboard a winged cloud,
I'll serenade the closing stanza to my beloved land;
to the dark shades in the jungles of Kenya and the Malaya;
to the iconic beacons built by the First of May;
to the green glee nights in the new China,
for which I play, out loud, a thousand hearty poems;
to my comrades in Asia;
to the Malaya and the vibrant Bandung.
. . . .
From each home, each alley,
we converge like the Asian winds,
like the war chants of the Maghreb armies.

Apart from Jayli and Taj, the Russian influence can be discerned in the works
of many other Sudanese poets, including Abdel Raheem Abu Zikra and Kamal
Elgizouli, both of whom spent years there. Abu Zikra studied Russian language
and literature in Moscow, while Kamal studied law and international relations
at Kiev State University. Abu Zikra translated extensively from Russian poetry,

particularly Pushkin and Mayakovski, and glimpses of those poets found their way to his own verse.

In 1989 Abu Zikra put a tragic end to a short, turbulent life by jumping from the thirteenth floor of the Russian Academy of Science building in Moscow. Almost three decades later, his shocking death, at the age of forty-six, remains an unraveled mystery. Abdel Goddous el-Khatim notes that the notion of death had haunted Abu Zikra's poetry since his early youth. His sole collection, *al-Raheel fil Layl* (Parting at Night), is replete with references to death.

> Death will come
> It will have your eyes
> This death is keeping our company
> day and night
> Sleepless, deaf
> like a veteran grief
> or a meaningless sin
> Your eyes, then, will be meaningless words
> a muffled cry, silence
> Silently, we will sink to the abyss.
>   ("al-Raheel fil Layl" [Parting at Night])

However, Jabir Hussain could identify two distinct voices in Abu Zikra's poetry. A highly optimistic, positive voice that marked his production during the 1960s and a melancholic voice that started to hold sway over the poet from the 1970s, leading to his tragic death in 1989.

The first era presents a cheerful voice, full of life and hope.

> Light illumed my window this morning
> It spilled its luminous water and crystals under the door
> It couldn't catch an inside view
> except a sigh of longing
> and me staring at the waking up windows
> to hear chatters around breakfast tables
> and at that point feel the bliss of life

soft and sweet, invading my ribs
In my rapture
I almost flew to embrace the buses, the pavement
swim in the green lake of a tree growing at my doorsteps
and drown myself in the dew of the eyes
of a girl with pretty eyes.
    ("Sabahiyah" [Morning])

That cheerful mood, according to Hussain, was by no means fanciful or dreamy. The poet remained sensitive to the people's needs and aspirations, closely attached to the poor, soothing their sufferings, and raising their morale.

If I owned this world
and if the powerful jinn soldiers of Solomon were still alive
I would order "Karima" to send me hills of fresh "gondaila" dates
I would order deliveries of ivory and beech
I would order the Kandakas [Kushite queens] to recall the legends of
    Meroe
I would run water springs for us to wash up
And would weave a bracelet of yearning
into a love poem for a face shining with beauty like a bright moon.
    ("Hob al-Fuqaraa" [My Beloved: The Poor])

In sharp contrast to the 1960s, his '70s poems were replete with gloomy ideas and skepticism.

Our old friends are pushing us towards suicide
They are no longer a source of inspiration
for perseverance
We vainly try to deceive them with false smiles
and narrow eyes, distracted looks
They have grown helpless
When we push on the button, we get nothing but the same laugh
The same story

The same debacle!

("Hadhadaat" [Soothing Voices])

Sufism, a deeply rooted practice in Sudan, has attracted a large number of poets. It is striking to note that Sudanese Sufi poetry has a unique African flavor. Scenes of the dervishes, in their colorful dresses, absorbed in their mystic rituals, and dancing to the rhythm of drumbeats bring forth a truly African atmosphere. Look at this stanza by Muhammad el-Fayturi.

In the solemn presence of my master,
my emotions are playing havoc with me.
Faceless, I gaze.
Legless, I dance.
My flags and drums packing the horizon.
My passion annihilating my passion.
My annihilation is engrossment.
I am your slave;
yet the master of all lovers.

("A Roaming Dervish's Stanza")

Sufism and Africa were two overriding themes in the poetry of el-Fayturi, who is particularly keen to present himself as a son of Africa. Out of his eight collections, three carried the name of the continent on the title: *Songs of Africa*, *A Lover from Africa*, and *Remember Me Africa*. African themes continued to feature heavily in most of his other collections.

Wake up, Africa
Wake up from your black dream
You have had a long sleep—Aren't you bored yet?
Aren't you bored of sitting at your master's feet?
How long have you lain down in the dark
exhausted, in your ailing hut
With pale longing
like an insane woman

building with her own hands the darkness of tomorrow
Hungry, chewing her remaining days
like a paralyzed cemetery guard!
   ("Al Ba'ath al-Afriki" [African Revival])

"The Signs Ode" (*Mu'allaqat al-Isharat*) by Muhammad Abdul-Hai is an example of philosophical Sufism. It is a compilation of seven pieces—each devoted to a prophet—running in a chronological order from Adam down to Muhammad. Philosophical Sufism was an important stage in Abdul-Hai's trajectory as a poet, which started with an earnest search for identity, the focus of his seminal work, *al-Awdah ila Sinnar* (Sinnar: A Homecoming).

In addition to identity and Sufism, patriotism and politics shine across this anthology. Himmaid, Kamal Elgizouli, Hashim Siddig, Aalim Abbas, Azhari Mohammed Ali, al-Saddig al-Raddi, Fidaili Jamma', and Mahjoub Sharif use fascinating allegories to convey feelings of frustration, hope, and dreams.

Pure romance is represented by two pieces from Idris Jamma'. The first, "In the Spring of Love," is a heartbreaking narrative of a broken love affair, while the second, "A Poet," tells why he thinks poets are the most miserable creatures on earth.

First, the maiden clay of agony was created.
Then in the fire of passion it was scorched.
And when providence called out: Be!
it transformed into a clay of misery: a poet; sculptor of words,

No one is more fascinated with the sea than Mustapha Sanad. He takes us on a dive into "The Old Sea."

Between us is the story of romance poets:
a cloud flirtatiously pressing her bosom against the translucent horizon.
That's me,
a coast-less sea,
a turbulent, obscure sea,
beginning-less, fathomless, ageless;

yet deep inside, I have a throbbing heart,
passionate and fervent.

In another piece, we watch as he spreads his violin bow across the night sea, in his desperate search for "The Lost Violins."

And I spread my violin bow—a bridge across the night sea,
then sank to the bottom:
swollen eyed, the drums of the bustling world bombarding my ears:
Feel sorry not for the bygone—
Some dwellings hold out; others drift away,
until distance brings them back to bay.

Rugaia Warrag and Najlaa Osman Eltom are two important female voices in the Sudanese literary arena since the 1990s. In the examples presented here, both poets address the theme of exile but from different perspectives. Rugaia's piece is an emotional account of a Sudanese girl in a western city where the sight of snow stirs in her feelings of estrangement and evokes vivid memories of the warmth of family and community. In that moment of overwhelming longing, she hears a familiar voice coming from within: *Wooooob! Wooooob*— the same scream that women in Sudan let out at moments of pain and loss. But here in this cold city, no one answered her distress call. Najlaa's story, on the other hand, is set at home, yet the same feeling of estrangement besets the young girl, a tea seller, as she struggles to earn a decent living against a cocktail of odds.

Najlaa and Rugaia represent a new wave of prose poets, a genre that is gaining mounting recognition as a powerful current in Sudan and the Arab world at large. That wave brought to light other female names, such as Iman Ahmad, Randa Mahjoub, Kaltoum Abdalla, Sara Hasabo, Iman Adam. These poets address a wide range of themes and pose a complex mixture of existential and philosophical questions.

In a country that hosted Africa's longest civil war, it is no wonder that the theme of war has featured heavily in post-independence Sudanese poetry. One poem that eloquently depicts the agonies of civil war is "On the Bank of

River Sobat" by Nylawo Ayul, a female poet from South Sudan, who writes in Arabic. Her birthplace in Upper Nile was at the heart of the decades-long hostilities between the two parts of the country, which eventually led in 2010 to its split into two independent states. Another poem by Ayul that is presented in this collection, "An Amulet for the Mango Tree," shows a melancholic scene of war.

A prolific poet is Rawda el-Haj, with five collections to her name. Her love poems are tender and outpouring, replete with poignant images.

Every day I get more convinced
that I was created for you alone.
It is through your eyes that I see the world;
On your lips my poems are born.
Without you,
my life is a wasteland.
I am colorless,
tasteless,
smelling like a land never visited by rain.
Every day I get more convinced
that I am a matchstick.
Only once it can ignite,
so be the one who lights me
and let me illuminate your fields at night.
No one but you knows the secret
of keeping my match alive
for long years to come—a full life.
No one but you
can lend life a beautiful color.
No one but you
can convince my heart,
the stubborn, skeptic heart of mine
to break the bad habit
of breaking away.
    ("Heart's Confessions")

There are scores of other female voices who write both classical and *taf'ila* poetry. A greater number of female poets write in the vernacular. Both dialect poetry and folk poetry have always been popular as they appeal to a much wider segment of the population, particularly the low educated who generally cannot fully appreciate poems written in standard Arabic. What adds to the appeal of these two genres is the fact that they are often communicated orally, intonated, and even put to music. While dialect poetry accounts for the vast majority of the entire mass of song lyrics, the popularity of folk poetry has reached new levels starting from the beginning of the new millennium, which saw a phenomenal rise in the use of mobile phones and satellite broadcasting. The wide public access to the Internet and online platforms enabled traditional forms of folk poetry, particularly *dubait* (quatrain) to spread beyond the Bedouin boundaries and establish a strong presence even in the capital. More interestingly, *dubait* and other forms of folk poetry are increasingly finding favor with even the younger generations of both sexes, and the language and cultural barriers that previously held these forms within their original boundaries are now fading away.

Today, satellite TV and radio programs on folk poetry are enjoying high viewership. Indeed, the strong interest of female poets in this genre is a continuation of a centuries-old tradition. Historically, women demonstrated superb skills in composing poems celebrating the heroism and chivalry of their sons and brothers who rose in defense of the tribe. Poems composed by such female names as Shaghaba in the sixteenth century and Banouna bitt al-Makk in the nineteenth century are popular songs today. Shaghaba was the mouthpiece of her tribe, the Kawahla, praising its heroes and even joining them in battle against enemies. She derided her own son for the lack of battle scars on his body.

I'm far from proud of you,
my son, Hussain;
Look at your bulging belly,
and your scratch-free skin!

No less vocal was Banouna, daughter of the chief of Jaalieen tribe. She could not live with the fact that her brother Ali, the battle-scarred hero, had to die "humbly" at home, with women around his bed wailing and pouring ashes on their hair. A knight like him deserved a glorious death.

> I will miss you, Ali,
> Will miss your head-chopping sword
> and your daring assaults, when you lead your brave cavalries in battle.
> But dying like this, amid wailings and ashes hurled on heads, is barely a
>   fitting end.
> A warrior like you deserves to die in battle, decorated with your blood
> with dead bodies scattered around, and dust high on the air

The poetry scene today is increasingly opening up to prose poetry like never before. Works of poets like Al-Saddig al-Raddi, Rugaia Warrag, Najlaa Osman Eltom, Nylawo Ayul, Khalid Hassan Othman, Hatim Al Kinani, Mamoun Eltilib, and others are gaining currency, particularly among the younger generations. This current is growing in strength and is poised to dominate the literary scene in the years to come.

This anthology is only a limited cross section of the colossal mass of poetry being produced in post-independence Sudan. It is unfortunate that only a little portion of it made its way beyond the Sudanese borders, to some Arab world's cultural capitals, such as Cairo and Beirut. Several factors stood in the way, notably the poor publishing industry and the fact that the majority of the poets could not afford to pay the costs of publishing abroad. Another reason, cited by notable critic Abdel Goddous el-Khatim, is that literary criticism had not built a sustainable flow that could serve as a solid platform for continuous critical discourse. Had we had such a platform, he argued, "We would not have needed to prove that al-Mahjoub was the first to write a foot poem in the Arab world, and that Muawia Mohammed Nour was the first to introduce the stream of consciousness into the modern Arab story. Nor would we have had trouble tracing the beginnings of cultural criticism in Sudan to the writings of Mohammed Ashri al-Siddig."

MODERN SUDANESE POETRY

My Beloved Aazza

KHALIL FARAH

Our passion for you, Aazza, is firm and stout.
Like mountains we stand, hard to sway.
Our bowstrings, alert and taut,
keep intruders away.
I never forsook my homeland: the land of ultimate beauty;
I always sought perfection, never rested for less.
My heart never throbbed for someone else;
as to the left I lean, take me in your right hand and embrace.
I can never forget Bilal's orchard
our playgrounds under the shade
like flowers on hilltops
leaping to reach the stars
a palm-frond crescent braided on my forehead.
Your chaste charm is a blessing on my heart;
the flames of your love are healing my wounds;
your conceit is innocent playfulness;
my tears as sweet as pure water;
I grow in awe of you,
as in grandeur every day you grow.
In Khartoum you come out;
from the groves of Shambaat you sprout.
Mountains guarding Omdurman
and deep in my heart I do find you,
a cure to my most stubborn ailment.
Staying all night awake,
counting stars on my camelback,
out of food, and of patience, I can't wait
to reunite with my gazelle-eyed back at home.

Wedding Parade

MUHAMMAD EL-MAHDI EL-MAGZOUB

In the heat of *daluka* drumbeats,
the young girls were casting charms,
from kohl-lined eyes,
where beauty felt at home.
Tonight, mother of the bride, we brought you
our cream of the cream;
palm fronds in our hands,
a good omen for green times to come.
Virgins as soft as young plants,
nursed in the shades for blooming time.
Rapture flying out of the drums,
like flocks of birds taking to the sky,
as the wedding parade gaily slid along the Nile bank.
We would catch rare glimpses of unguarded beauty,
yet we never go beyond the limits.
Tonight, mother of the bride, we brought you
our cream of the cream;
palm fronds in our hands,
a good omen for green times to come.
A proud community servant did the honors;
carrying around the incense burner,
barefooted, in brisk steps, all smiles, he warmly welcomed the parade.
An elated old woman recited warm-hearted verse,
her voice undulating, recalling past glories,
the girls clapping to the rhythm, while shooting glances around;
a mischievous gazelle straightened her dress,
behind others' backs, she showed me her necklace
a pigeon stepped forward, uncovered her hair,
and spread wings and chest,
exposing gleaming scars on the cheeks.

Tonight, mother of the bride, we brought you
a groom who is the cream of the cream;
the best match for a bride,
who is a queen among her maids;
a wellborn. A well-guarded pearl,
whose depths no diver dared to probe.
A broken-hearted sprang high.
A whip thundered on his shoulders as he landed.
He did not flinch, though;
for parting is more painful.
A highbred waiting for her long-awaited knight,
greeted him with a waft of fragrance from her braided hair;
an overt gesture but a short encounter,
and the beauty withdrew from the dancing circle.
With a shy smile,
she quickly took back in,
a mutinous finger that peeked out of her robe,
dusting my glances off her bracelets;
no communication allowed, I was warned.
Who would take me back to my playful days?
Who would save me from an exile,
that usurped my soul and lent me a false face?
I am craving for a sip from tattooed lips;
she could unveil her face to me
but would always keep a distance
and remain beyond my reach.
The norm of love in my country is constraint
and unfailing observance of chastity.
My whole heart is devoted to you, my homeland;
it never swayed westward or eastward.
I never shared the lust for prestige,
of my fellow civil servants;
among the ranks of the poor I shall proudly stay.
I long for my innocent village,

that knows nothing about my sufferings,
here in this alien city;
alone in a hotel with no neighbors around,
no relatives, or acquaintances;
swallowed in utter darkness;
climbing the rocky nights with a blind lantern;
longing for the deep massage of *dilka*,
the scent of *karkaar*,
and the silky *garmasis* gown;
watching the caravans of palm trees,
and the Nile as their escort and singer;
my water jar is full,
Treating myself to cold sips of Nile water,
from an engraved gourd utensil.

A Poet

IDRIS JAMMA'

Evoking embedded sorrows to endure the night's gloom
stirring imagination's flame
joining night's parades
whispering to ghosts and shadows.
Light enough to be swept away by a child's smile,
yet no might can shake him out of place.
Standing in awe before every trace of beauty,
and in everything he discerns a hidden grace.
A profligate who heeds no barriers;
a dervish in perpetual ecstasy and invocation.
First the maiden clay of agony was created.
Then in the fire of passion it was scorched.
And when providence called out: Be!
it transformed into a clay of misery: a poet; sculptor of words,
who joins the winds in songs,
to the delight of woods and mountains.
From each mound, he makes himself a platform, to recite his elaborate woes.
A child who builds dream castles in sands,
then tears down his dreams.
Like an aromatic wood,
burning itself to fragrance.

In the Spring of Love

IDRIS JAMMA'

In the spring of love we used to savor,
and sing and whisper;
chasing birds from one branch to another.
Then I lost pace with the past,
and sorrow engrossed deep at heart.
Two images in a heavenly stream, we cruised.
We sipped life's enchanting essence;
yet we are far from satiated.
That's love—never pose questions;
never blame us.
To heaven we were heading,
but we lost our way.
I lost pace with the past;
sorrow engrossed deep at heart.
My soul released long-held feelings.
I have dissolved my heart for you,
unto melodies and whimpering.
So have mercy on the *oud*,
when it sings me into a sad melody.
Your smiles are the only food and wine I have left.
One beaming smile of yours
can drive darkness away from my world
and bring water and blossom back to my desert.

Dig No Grave for Me

MOHAMMED EL-FAYTURI

When silence takes you far from us,
and you flicker in the distance,
like a caravan flag drowned in the sand—
the old words within us go green,
and the sacrificial fire on mountaintops whoops.
And you—our face hiding behind a thousand clouds—
keep running us around the corners of caves,
decorated with gloom.
And questions beget questions,
but the answer remains the same.
We call out your name.
We implant our voices like sandal trees around you
and run after funeral processions,
naked in death rooms.
We bring you the confident faces,
and the scared ones too.
We bring you our ancestors' amulets and invocations,
when blood collides against blood.
We bring you the swift Magian prayers;
the rituals of the tropics;
downpour at times of drought and barrenness;
the jungle, the river, and the storm!
From afar on horseback comes,
our long-awaited cavalier, with the golden spear.
O the cavalier of sorrow:
let your horses run their hooves on our savage graveyard.
Agitate its soil.
Take it off the death hooks.
Each death cloud that falls asleep on the earth's chest
is absorbed into the earth's womb,

where a baby revolution begins to form.
Pluck it off the death grip, O cavalier of sorrow.
Green:
An arch of fire and grass.
Green:
Your voice;
The flag of your face;
Your grave.
Dig no grave for me;
I shall lie in every inch of the earth.
I shall lie like water on the Nile's body;
like the sun over my homeland's fields.
The likes of me never take a grave for an abode.
They stood up,
and you stood up.
what makes the little tyrants think—and their faces grow pale—
that when the fighter dies so does the cause?
I know why tyrants believe in their guns.
I am not afraid—
My voice is the gallows for all tyrants—
Nor am I repentant;
my soul is boiling with rage.
Every tyrant is an idol, a wooden doll.
And you smiled . . .
All tyrants are dummies.
Perhaps it occurred to the idol; the tyrant doll,
as he decorated men's chest with death medals,
that he's the hero still.
And you walked up—in shackles.
Dig no grave for me;
I will climb to the gallows
and will shut the time's windows
behind me.
I will wash my head with blood;

I will chop my palm
and imprint it as a star on our time's façade,
over the leaning walls of its history.
I will sow my wheat for the birds and the passersby.
They killed me;
but my murderer-shivering, wrapped in my death shroud,
won't admit it.
But who am I?
I'm a man standing outside time's gate.
Each time they forge a fake hero,
with a broken heart I cry: O my beloved homeland.

A Roaming Dervish's Stanza

MOHAMMED EL-FAYTURI

My soul thinning out—to a twilight;
beaming with radiance and dew,
like a dervish clinging to his master's feet,
absorbed in woe;
my body aglow;
everyone else is blind: can't see me no matter how hard they hearken.
I am but a body; a stone,
some object across the street
isles drowned in seabed
a belated fire
a faint oil lantern
in a remote corner of a house—in Beirut
I glow for seconds, then wither and die.
What a shame! I'm stuttering my way to you, master
I am my grief in incarnation
I dissolve in you
Are you me?
The stretched hand yours or mine?
The voice: yours or mine?
Who is mourning who?
In the solemn presence of my master,
my emotions are playing havoc with me.
Faceless, I gaze.
Legless, I dance.
My flags and drums packing the horizon.
My passion annihilating my passion.
My annihilation is engrossment.
I am your slave;
yet the master of all lovers.

Yaaqut al-Arsh

MOHAMMED EL-FAYTURI

A world owned not by its owners;
its richest are its masters: the poor.
The losers are those who take not what it shyly gives out.
The senseless are those who take things at their face value.
The crown of a tyrant sultan is an apple,
dangling from the plaza flagpole.
The crown of a Sufi,
on a straw mat gleams.
Believe me, O Yaaqut al-Arsh,
the dead are not those dead
nor happiness is that one.
Which seas of the world are you asking about, dearest?
About a whale with feet cast of rock
and eyes of corundum?
About clouds made of fire?
Islands of corals?
About a dead man carrying his own corpse,
running to his death place?
Don't be surprised, O Yaaqut:
More magnificent than man's destiny is man himself.
The judge curling his moustaches, flirting with the pub singer.
The village's wise man is hanged,
and the monkeys ramping in the marketplace.
Dearest:
Copper is as precious as gold in the eyes of the destitute.
Your judge, tied to his stolen seat,
issuing verdicts
and swaggering across the cemetery.
Only through our own eyes can you see us.
You can't recognize us,

unless we draw you in close enough
and we open up.
Our lowest in rank, O Yaaqut,
may well ascend to the top;
so choose the rock-bottom,
to get to the highest point.
The seawater has dried up.
The bird troops called off their journey;
the perforated sieve is on your shoulders.
Mountains of grief in your eyes.
Don't cry, dearest;
We both have had enough;
the grand grief is too good for words.

Migrating from Sai

JAYLI ABDEL RAHMAN

The women piled up on the shore
like heavy memories on the heart
of a heartbroken poet.
They kissed my mother's face
and waved to the loaded boat.
My uncle was wetting my tiny head,
with incessant flow from his gaping, deep-set mouth.
His coarse beard was pricking my cheek;
his moustache flirting with my eyelids;
his tears flowing copiously down his cheeks.
"Son,
if you get there safely
and all went well,
tell your father to think of his brother,
to remember him, despite the distance."
Old men on the shore,
under the shade of palm trees standing,
like ghosts of a satirical myth,
narrated to the shores by the raging waves.
An old man gazing at the bystanders;
and beyond the palm trees,
feeble houses ghostly flittering on the horizon.
As the sails soared,
so did wailing and whimpering.
Eyes overflowed with hot tears.
My uncle was waving both hands;
and my mother responding with broken glances.
Like a fleeting idea,
the parade sailed from sight.
The child's heart was pounding with excitement

his mother was adding melody and tone to his dreams:
In Egypt one finds orange fruit
and delicacies of all sorts,
palaces craning to the sky,
the whole of Egypt dancing,
under alluring lights.
I set about coloring this fantasy,
with the creative brush of my dreams
adding shades to my father's beautiful picture
stored in my mind.
The train let out loud whistles
I ran and my mother scurried off
lending fun to the clamor.
We boarded the train. What a pleasure!
I lost myself in watching the green fields.
They seem endless those fields.
So perplexing! Can trees really run?
Filled with excitement I asked my mother,
but only received a curt answer.
What a night!
full of hugs and tears.
And oh, my uncle!
He died there,
on a heap of debris.
We mourned him here.
We set up a funeral in our hearts.
And in chest bones torn with grief,
we engraved letters to serve,
as beacons for estranged souls.
From our parents' mouths we were fed flaming songs
full of perseverance and promise,
that one day we will come back to you, Saai;
to rebuild our shacks and alleys.

The Wharf and the Walkway Rhythms

Your green shade is abundant and inviting.
Your eyes offering dozens of quays.
Your lighthouses guiding all-night cruisers that go astray.
You incomer, escorted by the wind's cavalry to the jubilant harbor;
silence foliates, extends its tents,
when utterances fall into the bottom,
the color in the singer's throat dries up;
and the rhythm, the features, and the make-ups all wither and die.
The façades look like stony faces,
like pagan icons,
for the glad tidings that once pervaded the harbor's air
are now sipped off by the wind,
which kept beating its hollow drum all night long,
dropped the pyramid stone on the skylight,
and seeded barrenness across pathways.
O incomer,
We have nothing to offer;
We are in the background of the picture: a light or a color;
An ebony frame embroidered with carvings and decorations.
Our sole asset is we sing for the wind.
One day, all the flexible bells tolled.
It strutted to the harbor on board the wind's mail.
The sea whales tore down its blue flag.
We saw its masts fall down into a fathomless abyss,
yet every day we stand by the dock in wait;
we ask the harbor, the lighthouses, and the waves.
We never forgot. In the night's shrine we planted cactus trees,
erected a sign on its solid trees,
and built a fence of flowers and stars.
At night, when our face soaked in the city's grapevine bounces back to us,

we chew colocynth and bitter memories;
we sing under the wind's ceiling,
for the lanterns that smile to the walkways;
we watch the harbor and the distant lighthouses,
and sing.
O incomer,
we have nothing to offer;
our sole asset is we sing for the wind.

The Horse and the Wind

MOHYIDDIN FARIS

The memory was shattered.
The placenta gave birth to a graveyard.
The local midwife was besieged by the wind in the rainy night.
Where are the birth ceremonies? I asked the bush foreteller.
I can't see any traces of slaughtered sheep's blood decorating the gate;
or any glow on the eyes of the censer,
on the city's doorsteps.
Silence reigned, and dark jargon filled the air;
the new seasons are being born;
the bush foreteller descends from the mount of silence,
ignites all lanterns,
and embeds all evenings with light;
the victims rise, dressed in purple, their daring eyes deriding calamities.
The prophecy goes:
On an ebony black horse he comes,
outracing light,
penetrating the veil of wind,
wearing the night as a shield;
he carves the face of identity,
and skins pawnbrokers.
The peels of words sing out;
the sun confiscates them,
but they confiscate her golden howdah,
and braid her hair into a guillotine,
to shear off the necks of the old times,
and open up our locked doors.
In the fire froth, I saw you,
a ruby that breastfed from the suns,
sipped from the nectar of cultures,
and reclined on the world's forehead.

Thieves took shelter under her nets,
then hastily spread their ladders.
So unsheathe your sword.
For all discourses are still mere fallacies;
all deities are busy fighting each other;
and those dressed in saint mantel
are owls perched on the world's wreckage.
The ships are neighing for departure;
let go of me!
The sea has a refreshing smell;
my ships are neighing for departure;
the winds have inflated the sails;
this city eats its offspring,
then hides in the darkness.

Homeland

MOHYIDDIN FARIS

For the first time,
I feel I am a freeman, in a free homeland;
the shackles that have long festered my hands
are now corroded chains under my feet.
The land of treasures, my land,
will soon open its gates to light,
when dawn spreads its wings
and drops its shawl on the river's shoulders.
Even the fetuses are confident and happy,
in the comfort of their wombs.
I could hear their twitter in the darkness.
Even the whining of waterwheels,
that long tormented my ears,
is now sweet tunes.
Lively songs are now shining,
even in the eyes of the crippled elderly.
My homeland, the land of treasures, has blossomed
like fragrance gliding down from the lips of rosebuds,
like a pearl on the coast,
like the wings of perfume flickering to the embrace of the soft breeze.
For the first time,
I feel I am free—my homeland is free;
my sky is free;
no alien birds bugging its stars,
or specters of clouds.
The road we once paved with skulls
will now be washed with fragrance
and embedded with rosebuds
and pigeons' twitter
when dawn spreads its wings

and drops its shawl on the shoulders of the river.
My homeland, the land of treasures,
is extending a hand from the heart of stars,
clean as a pure heart,
to every nation through rugged mountains rising to the wellspring.
a song from the south to embrace an Asian song.
Our windows are open;
so come dawn,
and throw down your white and violet braids,
and on the doorsteps sprinkle your lovely songs.

An Afro-Asian Song

TAJ EL-SIR EL-HASSAN

When I play our ancient songs, O my heart,
as dawn lands on my chest aboard a winged cloud,
I'll serenade the closing stanza to my beloved land;
to the dark shades in the jungles of Kenya and the Malaya;
to the iconic beacons built by the First of May;
to the green glee nights in the new China,
for which I play, out loud, a thousand hearty poems;
to my comrades in Asia;
to the Malaya and the vibrant Bandung.
O Dien Phu,
our land is craving for light and blooms.
The scene of the castle is still fresh in my eyes;
dead bodies of the enemy hanging down from the blue rocks.
O Dien Phu.
I've just seen a soldier embroidered in blood,
his rose-red heart lying in the open—
a Parisian who met a humiliating death,
in Dien Phu.
Little I know, comrades;
for I haven't been to Indonesia—
the land of Sukarno.
Nor have I seen Russia.
Yet from the luminous heart of the new Africa,
where darkness is sipping trickles of light from distant stars,
I can see the people in the heart of the Malaya,
like the iconic beacons built by the First of May;
just as vividly as I can see Jomo,
rising up as genuine as dawn light.
O flowery forests of Kenya;
O stars looming as beacons;

21

O Algeria;
here the triumphant arch takes its proud shape.
From each home, each alley,
we converge like the Asian winds,
like the war chants of the Maghreb armies.
O Egypt: my country's full sister,
as sweet as your springs, luxuriant as your verdant meadows;
what an eternal truth you are.
O Egypt: mother of Sabir.[1]
My heart is so full of you, O sister of my motherland.
Let's wipe off the enemies from our valley;
our friends are stretching hands:
The face of Gandhi and resonant echoes of the fathomless India.
The voice of Tagore, the chanter,
his verse flying around an art grove.
O Damascus:
we are all united in aspiration.[2]
O vanguard comrades, leading my people to glory,
your candles are soaking my heart in green light.
Haven't you heard the voice of "Taiwan" from afar coming?
Giving new life to the people,
or seen the face of Joudeh?[3]
Faces to us returning from prison,
faces shaking hands with us,
faces returning to live anew
in Gezira, their mother island.
The souls of "Joudeh" are surely not dead.
O my comrades:
to Wahran our friends are marching,
and in my blood the Canal[4] is running—
free as a bird.
In the heart of Africa I stand in the vanguard,
and as far as Bandung my sky is spreading.
The olive sapling is my shade and courtyard,

O my comrades:
O vanguard comrades, leading my people to glory,
your candles are soaking my heart in green light.
I'll sing the closing stanza,
to my beloved land;
to my fellows in Asia;
to the Malaya,
and the vibrant Bandung.

The Exile and the Kingdom

I never left my father's home,
to live in a desert cave,
covered up in a fabric woven by the wind
on the loom of silence.
Feeding from the Lord's Table;
and keeping my ears pricked up and my eyes raised at high mast,
hoping a foal would emerge out of the wilderness,
and, in the blink of an eye, we transcend the bounds,
to the hereafter and the realm of revelation.
And on coming back I reveal to you the secrets of the transfiguration.
I swear by the gray streaks on my father's hair,
and by my mother's honor,
that the Lord's Angel has visited me at night,
split open my chest,
immersed his fingers in a sea of blood,
plucked out fear and the wind of doom,
untied my tongue,
baptized me,
wiped my forehead, and rid me of the shackles of poverty and time.
I would tell you things beyond intellectual prowess, and intrigue,
that I was on the fringe of eternal bliss,
in the arms of the eternal twilight,
I was served wine in silver glasses from the hands of eternally young boys.
My drinking companions were messengers from the east and the west.
Our singing voices never waned;
we never felt drained.
And because wine there was running in streams;
and because houri girls—virgin and with wide, lovely eyes—
were coming and going, skirt-free,

I could not resist the temptation of the shade:
I was expelled.
My glorified abode: my father's home:
My cradle, my exile, my kingdom,
where I had endured the mysterious taboo,
and now came down to baptize you.

A Drib of Your Nectar

MOHAMMED EL-MAKKI IBRAHIM

My Lord!
What a charming blend you are,
Oh my *Khilassiyah*![1]
A tavern in clean sand carpeted;
eyes kohl-rimmed;
a figure from a lyric's hair braided.
A rose soaked in color.
I am but a drib of your nectar;
you are the orange.
Your thighs are brimming with *Khilassi* offspring.
Partly a Negro you are.
Partly an Arab—and for sure,
some of my words before the Lord.
He who buys you
will buy up the clove's fragrance from an evening's breath,
the coasts from an island's waist,
an island's waist from the ocean waves,
and the morning's bosom.
He who buys you
will buy a sheath for all wounds,
an elegy for all sorrows.
He who buys you
will buy from me and you,
the legacies of tear-shedding,
and ages of slavery.
He who buys you
will buy me, oh my pretty blend.
But am I going to sell my face,
and my words before my Lord?
Let them ask palm trees if they've ever seen sands like yours,

elegantly washed and sparkling clean.

Let them ask the sea if a nymph has, ever, in her wildest of dreams,

worn the faintest traces of your grace.

Let them ask the waves of invaders,

if they happened to meet in battle as bold and fearless as you,

like the Mahdist days.

Let them ask:

Every dove will intone,

graceful verse,

in praise of your bosom at dawn.

Let them ask:

The sword and the books will have a lot to tell.

They wanted to sip you off,

my orange,

so wombs of casks and vats should run out of nectar.

They strived to desecrate all sanctuaries,

so depravity should thrive.

But they are gone now,

leaving behind

the cask and the flask.

Your grapevines still prolific, fruit-laden;

and brim-full glasses still being passed round.

Shake up the spring's trunk,

and wash up,

of your sorrowful past,

in visions and perseverance.

Shake up the castles' towers.

The bees have roamed the meadows,

and greeted you with fresh nectar.

The red east is bathing in virgin sunshine.

And you are draped in vigor.

We speed our way ahead,

while others drag their feet,

to bring our race to the finish line.

Your admirers lose themselves to slumber.
Only in their dreams can they catch a glimpse of you.
Old fronds are motionless.
Seabirds in utter silence.
The spring has dozed off and everyone is sound asleep,
except me,
the fragrance,
and the spears of your vigilant guards.
When I get through,
I race down to you;
my hair wet;
my chest full of flowers.
So keep your door ajar,
and your bed warm.
Put on a nightgown weaved of fragrance,
and songs of the spring and the trees.
I have a lengthy chat,
with your bosom at dawn.
Alas, my orange,
love encounters are short-lived.
So come feast your eyes on me—
Dawn will break soon.
The ocean is peaceful and serene,
palm fronds caressing and romancing,
the palace pool lush with water lilies,
and the bees showering flower buds with kisses.
Now I am elegant like never before,
more vigorous than vigor,
glittering in the attire of new light.
So feast your eyes on me,
before the next tide drifts me away.
But I shall soon come back aboard a fresh wave.
Have you recognized me?
on winds and waves;

On heavy rains;
in my death and resurrection,
I shall come.
Say, then, you have recognized me
and have engraved my features and genes
on rock and sand, between groves.
Say my name is on the love plaque now embossed.
Now it's time to leave—
though I still crave,
for the bounties of your body;
still unquenched of your bosom.
So promise to call me in again,
to your bed for yet another night,
and to make it particularly long,
with your hair on my arms;
your color dissolved in my color and genes;
I am dissolved in you.
So blend me,
with the graves of tropical flowers,
with the tearful times,
and ages of slavery.
Embrace my remains and let the sap
carry me along, in its life cycles, across the island.
Embrace my remains and
hold me tight in your arms.
What a pleasant fragrance!
How fecund you are!
Negro and naked!
And—for sure,
some of my words before the Lord.

A Farm on the Hill

MOHAMMED EL-MAKKI IBRAHIM

Before you were born,
and became a farm on the hill,
you used to be a sanctuary for foxes,
taking shelter from the foothill dogs;
a haven for birds,
weaving their nests on treetops.
Heaven's water,
would year after year moisten your cheeks
and drape a green shawl on your shoulders.
In summer they would come,
to feast their axes on your flesh.
You would hold out,
standing as firm as faith,
little bothered by the hovering death,
the lashes of the scorching sun and wind,
rocks on your chest: weighty and burning.
You never groaned
never uttered a blasphemous word.
That was before we met;
before you became a mother and a field.
Before summer departed.
I combed your hair,
rolled rocks off your shoulders,
built a perimeter fence
and an embankment.
I dug a well,
set the soil for plantation,
ran streams length and breadth,
and set up a shade for our nap.
The sun, meanwhile, stood high up,

at the sky pole,
spilling its heat over the stones.
The winds kept sharpening their nails,
and slapping the hill on the face.
The huge sky was hollow and barren;
the rainy season nowhere in the horizon.
That particular summer,
I gave a solemn pledge:
I won't let them touch a single hair
of your dangling hair plaits.
If they were to come at dawn,
I shall be waiting for them.
If they chose to visit under night's cover,
they would be fended off by the fence and words of God.
You must be in for a date with the rain, the plain thought,
seeing how beautiful you looked, like a bride in her wedding procession,
envied by the girls of the foothills,
and the girls of the hill cliffs as well.
Word among folks in the bush is:
the birds are roaming every corner, gathering fabrics for your wedding dress,
painting flowers and spike,
on your palms.
The clouds, the word goes,
are forming a permanent shade over our heads,
a shield against the midday sun's rage.
At night, they send you dewdrops,
aboard rose-colored parachutes,
landing on your bosom's runway,
or falling out on the moon's belt.
It then falls into my conscious mind
that you are a virgin,
reclining on the sand velvet
at the incline.
Your bosom breathless;

your dress unbuttoned—
in wait for the rain;
that you are the mother of my love's kids
and my farm on the hill.
Now I am certain,
if it rained,
and the land put on a false green mantel,
you will look fruit-laden and will turn
into a garden of fruits and flowers.
In summer,
when it's dry everywhere
and the land shivers in panic,
you will remain lush green,
perfectly beautiful,
fruit-laden.
You will remain,
my farm on the hill.

Two Love Poems and a Carnival

MOHAMMED EL-MAKKI IBRAHIM

The lover puts his palm to the local fortune-teller,
"O fortune-teller," he says,
reaching out to her with a silky cloud, a poet's cradle,
and a field full of stars:
"Tear up the veils of time;
break down the gates of the unknown;
unwrap its reticence and solitude."
She rocks and probes the palm laid peacefully on her lap,
after moments of bafflement and surprise,
she starts to tell the lover her reading of the story,
the story of my heart,
and my love to its sweetheart self:
Your palms are two poems: of love and carnival
two pillows soaked in ambergris,
spills of honey, wine, and jasmine.
Your palms are protecting my life and history.
When they land on my hand,
my hand will bloom and
create new deities and a virgin world.
And when they caress my forehead,
my forehead is relieved
of fever and stupor.
If on the heart they land and hearken,
they lend its beats wildness, glow, and vigor,
and it goes on beating forever.
Yesterday, when we bid farewell,
looking at me, two stars exchanged winks.
The solemn Nile jokingly cleared his throat.
A flirting star congratulated me.
"You are matchless," said the street.

Tell me, sweetheart:
When and how our affair came to be known?
Was the jasmine by the corner snooping on us?
and it carried the aroma of our conversation in her fragrance?
Did I whisper it to the Lord in a serene dawn?
Did we impart our secret to a young palm tree—and she got pollinated,
And gave birth to pearls and amber?
Did I intone it to a singer?
Perhaps it was me!
Or perhaps us!
I think, sweetheart, it is our love that is exposing us!

Songs for October

(1) Martyr

MOHAMMED EL-MAKKI IBRAHIM

In his village,
he was the sorghum field,
brimming with heavily laden stalks.
The cotton field,
blooming with luminous bolls.
He was twenty,
yet to see a thousand suns still heading his way;
yet to taste the bliss of marriage.
He was unarmed,
except for a chant on his lips,
and a stone on his hand.
He was at the frontline,
leading the way.
A shot was fired;
a bath of blood poured.
Out of his fellows' arms he slipped away.
His blood scented the ground, sending quivers on the soil veins.
An approaching dawn bolted back; his hair went gray.
The night's hair split into two braids.
The stars and embryos shockingly watched: hair-raised.
The breeze of heavens gracefully blew on his face.
The cart horses exchanged neighs,
flapping their wings in praise.
Thus,
on a soft feather cushion,
his chaste soul ascended,
to a hero's welcome in eternity.
There, he was celebrated
as a revolutionary,
a leader of martyrs,
an icon of sacrifice and patriotism.

(2) The Green October

Your name, a synonym of triumph,
is blossoming in people's hearts,
injecting faith and good omen;
a scarf wrapped around the jungle and the desert,
and a torch in our hands, and a weapon.
Armed with October,
we won't flinch; won't step back an inch.
We'll hit on rocks until they give birth to plants and greenery.
We will stay the course of glory,
until our name is entered in the book of eternity.
The land is singing your green name, O October
The fields have burst into wheat, promise, and hopes
and the land, its troves flung open, is chanting:
With your name's blessing, the masses have made it to victory,
the jail walls are down
and the chains are bracelets dangling
from a bride's wrist!

October has been in our nation,
since the dawn of history.
Behind the veils of sorrow and grief,
it lurked, steadfast and alert.
At the break of dawn out it came,
setting fire on history,
and setting itself aflame.
October was present in our early upheaval
with al-Makk al-Nimir.
It was the green swords in demonstrators' hands.
It was with al-Mazz, in his heroic stance.
And now once again it responded to Gorashi's call,
leading us to victory.

The Old Sea

MUSTAPHA SANAD

Between us walls expand—
as does an eternal night—
and a thousand doors stand.
Between us my senescence is laid bare,
and the masks of youth fade away.
What would people say,
when aging palms frivolously swing and sway,
and ruin reins over the land again?
A virgin land's lust for rain,
triggered by glittering mirage echoing
down rivulets' veins!
Your radiant features crossed my mind's window.
I called out: I wish you were still here,
offering your light to the wind, to the night and shadow,
and the lightning to me, the thunderstorms,
and the long-paced, flying clouds,
satiating the flames under my scorched ribs,
and persistently asking:
Why should you leave at night,
with no bags or raincoat?
Peeking through office corridors, black shelves,
and old, frayed papers.
Your forgotten face crucified on the old staircase;
a pale trace—like a faint spark on firewood.
How could you leave, O crucified,
like grave signs by the corner of the road?
The clouds subsided and your image was back again,
sprinkled by the lightning's palm,
when flashes came in tandem,
and thunderstorm sparks went loose.

It blossomed then flew,
in redolent lilies with cheeks like a brilliant dawn.
The mirrors' throat rang like a bell,
and millions of necklaces fell apart.
Whenever I tried to come closer,
colors shied away,
and ice windows toweringly stood on the way.
I am a roamer carried on wind back,
met at each door with an injurious remark.
Between us my claws are exposed,
and blood runs down the corner of my jaws.
A true monster:
a ghoul: sinister, in a howling rage.
My coffins replete with death powder.
My tunnels home to winter reptiles set free.
My talisman:
a dough of the Lote tree,
a whale tooth,
a mummy.
Between us is what is visible to passersby:
a cliff of a far-off coast and a chestnut flower,
on the sands sitting close together,
leaving the universe in awe,
and the fields in shivers.
How come you seek refuge in idols mired in stinky mud?
when you are the source of vigor,
the essence of blossoming—
and yet you seem to prize the time-scarred,
the grave of oblivion.
Between us extends the lengthy route,
from spring to autumn.
Your abode is above the illusionary mansions,
while I take the floor dust for a night bed.
They dressed you in a silk gown—soft,

with rhyming swish,
and proclaimed you the crown of grace,
pride of grace,
glory of grace,
sun of grace,
grace of grace;
injected in your veins the essence of deceit.
Your love has set my heart on fire;
rib-torn, blood-stained, I remain.
Between us is the story of romance poets:
a cloud flirtatiously pressing her bosom against the translucent horizon.
That's me,
a coast-less sea,
a turbulent, obscure sea,
beginning-less, fathomless, ageless;
yet deep inside, I have a throbbing heart,
passionate and fervent.

The Lost Violins

MUSTAPHA SANAD

And I spread my violin bow—a bridge across the night sea,
then sank to the bottom:
swollen eyed, the drums of the bustling world bombarding my ears:
Feel sorry not for the bygone—
Some dwellings hold out; others drift away,
until distance brings them back to bay.
Learn alone how to stare at the glowing sun and copper eyes—
    dazzling mirrors
but our sober night,
and evening terrace,
stand like curtains over your eyes, over your weary lids.
Revelation exudes its violet fragrance,
and the stars turn verdant,
bestowing you with ultimate elegance,
with blue shadows,
with melodies that dance in rhythm with the wind,
with chants and hymns of the wilderness,
with hours for verse to run its course,
in them pour out its essence,
and milk its stabbed heart onto its routes to satiate their thirst.
I call out: You who are pouring forth like rainfall
don't you recall our times together?
In a field of ember we've been waiting for you, burning our lily years in
    sacrifice,
but you decline our offering.
Perhaps, O night torment, you used to visit us against our will,
then leave before you arrive,
as we, our nerves ripped apart, overhear the harbingers of fate,
behind the curtains of silence,
watching the birth scene, the lightning of our redemption

40

flickering between clouds of sighs.

Stand up and spread your presence in all directions,

like the old days, when your face was in control of all routes.

I'm deprived of your world, my vision blurred, in maze engrossed.

From my heart I served people my lifelong harvest, the concentrate of
   my grieved veins,

in cups made of light.

In my joy I go about kissing everyone on the road, even the houses' eyes,

the husky voice of my lost violins is roaring in night's seas, roaring like
   waterfalls.

Departure at Night

ABDEL RAHEEM ABU ZIKRA

You who's parting at night,
alone, alienated:
yesterday the firstlings of autumn visited me,
washed me with snow
and with meadows' brilliance.
You who's parting at night:
when the firstlings of autumn visited me,
my summer was stagnant,
my forehead cold,
and my silence lurking
behind woody houses.
Hiding its confusion in trees,
in the sinking rivers,
and the retracted vision.
The firstlings of autumn waved at me for a while,
when we moved away,
then they returned to me.
When they returned,
the wind jumped on my excited sails,
the heavenly sun beamed on my isolated corridors,
and I found myself in a long embrace with the springy sun
that never embraced me
in the early time,
the absent, improvised time.
Wait for me;
for I am traveling at night too,
alone, setting off on a long journey.
In the remote passageways wait for me.
In the desert highlands and by the sea
wait for me.

In the flapping of wings
and the routes of the migrating birds,
when the orbits collapse
and the sky grows gloomy and dark,
wait for me.

The Night Girl

ABDEL RAHEEM ABU ZIKRA

When she turned in,
all the neon lights suddenly glowed.
Outside the café, the downpour stopped
and so did the chatting.
On the way to the cups, the tea jug froze.
Amid the utter silence, a glass exploded on the tile floor.
The waiter turned his head, but his eyes got stuck in transit:
A girl!
O my Lord!
Your protection,
for the blooming eyes
for the flowing braids.
What a beauty! What a vigor!
Blessed is the Creator!
Those eyes flew down,
tearing off the stillness of the place.
The clients darted under the overflowing braids,
coaching themselves on the fragrance of her rain-wet dress.
No. That's not the right way!
The eyes nearly bruised her perplexed lids,
and her hair that was running away from the wailing wind and rain
was surprised to find the wind and the rain right here.
The wind was blowing on the café from all directions.
May the Lord who raised the heaven and fixed it in place
protect this captivating brilliance,
desperately seeking warmth despite the siege of these eyes!
And she slid back to the rain.
Silence reined for a minute
then the café retained its din and dust;

the waiter wiped off beads of sweat
and started to collect the broken glass fragments.
The jug came to its senses
and started anew pouring tea onto cups.
Outside, it started to rain again!

Who Triggered the Stone's Tongue?

ALI ABDEL QAYYOUM

A tap on the stone's shoulder
softened its neck muscles.
It turned its head, raised its eyes, scanning the horizon.
Another tap,
followed by a tender sigh,
taught it how to smile.
An affectionate gesture,
taught it how to talk.
After a brief stutter,
it managed to greet back.
Tell me, slick stone of alabaster,
how passion turned you silk soft?
Whose love turned your rock into a fountain?
causing the stream to dance and swing!
Tell me, son of the awesome rocks,
who illuminated your forehead with lightning?
Who opened up routes for rain through you?
I wonder who
decorated the earth with glory
under the transparent light?
I wonder who freed you, O rock,
from the bonds of the inanimate yoke?
Who triggered your tongue,
O rock,
my despair-engulfed silence,
who on earth triggered your tongue?

The Signs Ode

MUHAMMAD ABDUL-HAI

1. AN ADAMIC SIGN

With the Names,
we recall the world from its chaos:
The sea. The desert.
The stone. The wind. The water.
The trees. The fire. The female.
Darkness and light.
And then Allah will come,
wrapped in His divine attributes—the Names.
That's the birth of His vision.

2. A NOAHIC SIGN

I almost cry in the Lord's face,
how did You find peace,
after unleashing the water's terror
onto fields where, year after year,
sweaty work snatched a slice of greenness
off the jaws of the lion of barrenness?
Why should another wandering begin again?
But I say, as everything is fading away:
flash, O lightning, through the darkness of His agony
to illuminate this poem:
An ark, pregnant with all our weaknesses
and longing for our old new land.

3. AN ABRAHAMIC SIGN

Is he coming?
Is he coming through the night of utterance?
Through the silence of utterance and the starry rose,
in the night's core,

glittering like a sword in the flesh of darkness?
Is your other angel coming tonight? Listen!
a falcon's screech, wild glad tidings.
Foam of a slaughtered sheep's blood in the constellation of stars.
Luminous horses in the clouds,
a language in the wind made of green flames on trees,
the escaping night bird turning to ashes
in the mirrors of fire.

4. A MOSAIC SIGN

The ashes,
in the virgin dawn come together and mount,
green trees in the pure light,
red fruits in the dewy leaf,
a white bird, a lavish spring,
everything,
a dream revealing the promised land.

5. A JESUS SIGN

Here comes the tinkling of dawn's footsteps on hills and trees,
telling how the wind passed through the harp,
how the angel and the Virgin embraced,
under the ceilings of fire
and the street's din and dust—
and then they parted:
to his heaven, and to her subdued body,
and the blood song flashing in the bird's chords was put on play.

6. A MUHAMMADAN SIGN

The garden took us by surprise.
In its heart clusters of roses and fire transformed into light;
white, luminous horses;
peacocks on the land of soberness spread woven feather.
Everything on the leaves of truth:

Fire trees and a wave in deep seas,
of flame, of beauty and blessing.
The birds fall before reaching the shores,
joyfully embracing their burning fate.
The blooming garden took us by surprise.
At its heart the green dome blossomed,
and glad tidings flowed in: the chosen one was born; felicity became
　　reality,
dressed in fresh light from the sun,
the Names sang in celebration.

7. A SIGN

A sun of grass and two doves,
singing.
Before the beginning of time.
After the end of time.
Burning,
on the branches,
of ban trees.

Encounter

KAMAL ELGIZOULI

In the late hours of the night,
off the fence of the Grand Mosque,
a male leper, shabby and frail,
stealthily creeps onto the bosom of a fellow leper
just as shabby and frail,
and they embrace.
With palms as camel's hoofs
and three timber-dry arms,
they embrace,
in the wee hours of the night,
off the fence of the Grand Mosque.
But the last passerby,
who airs his belly on the floor
and goes on his way,
is too drunk and drowsy to see
he has just blown off an intimate moment—
bitterly fought for.

Whispers

KAMAL ELGIZOULI

It's not murder that I dread.
Not even a tragic end.
Nor this door being blown down outright,
or them storming in at midnight,
their naked guns in full sight.
No.
Not festering wounds, streams of blood,
or the wall dotted with fragments of my skull.
What I fear the most, I have to say,
is fear per se:
that devious and elusive thing,
that in a twinkling
can sneak in,
whispering deluding excuses—temptingly fancy,
while stealthily injecting weakness and despondency
into the inner pores of my soul.
That elegant, eye-catching thing
luring me into watching its glaring blade.
And once, for a second or two,
I am dazzled by the glow,
it slips in,
splitting me into two:
A half up there—in its illusionary world,
dying twice.
And a half down here,
half dead.
You are destined to die—and so are they;
No one is exempt.
So voice your rejection right here!

Out there, your defiant voice will come out,
pretty strong and vocal.
Die here,
to live there!

A Cell the Size of New Year's Eve

When I saw you,
landing like a dewdrop,
on the edge of the upper louver,
with your sweet glimmer,
jolting the stillness of silence,
clearing my darkness,
and dealing a sudden punch to my dream,
like a weed blade,
on New Year's Eve,
shoving its way through my ribs;
when I saw you,
the old longing invaded me,
like a glittering, dewy child,
sneaking behind bells and guards cast in their uniform,
arresting the harsh voice up on the fence,
paralyzing the baton and the rifle,
and on the glimmering wave of surprise,
she comes hopping,
one hop toward you,
a second toward me.
And when you gleamed,
like an ember,
on the ceiling of my cell,
millions of pictures
awakened my nerves, and distant memories;
and I craved,
for the laden, dewy leaves;
for your daring eyes
that always shrugged off danger;
and I wished we were together,

behind the grip of fences and time,
buying two seats,
on the flight feathers of a bird,
and arm in arm taking off,
to the sun airport,
or to the moon harbor.
If a single night could pass,
with no interrogation, apprehension;
no heavy feet chasing us along the sidewalk;
no sniffer dogs on our heels;
no search beneath our skins,
for white and red blood cells,
on our nerves for traces of the bow
and fingerprints of the string!
You would hide your intimate face inside me,
like a warm star I, too,
hide your intimate face inside me.
Yes! Like a warm star, not a light drizzle
that pours down for a minute or two
then calls off.
No. Rather like a star-oh!
a star full of warmth and vigor.
We would break the jar of the night,
sprinkle the fragments on the shore,
and disturb the serenity
of the Nile,
the pebble,
and the sand.
And we would on the waves carpet ride,
like two peaceful sparrows,
or fly around the city's dome
like two white pigeons.
We would spread love songs
at the gates of the grief-stricken alleys.

Love is the most precious thing we can offer
to the grief-stricken alleys.
We would quarrel in a flash,
and the next flash come back,
and break into giggles;
stick our tongues out at boredom
from rooftops
and tree branches.
Are you the one inhabiting my soul?
Or is it the salty sea, sweetheart?
Or are we both inhabited by perils?
When I saw your sudden landing
on my cell's window
like a gray sparrow,
I went toward you,
braving the guard,
and the rifle,
and, like your eyes, braving all perils.

Monologue

KAMAL ELGIZOULI

Under a waning moon suspiciously looking down at us
and faint glimpses of a lonely star,
fast heading to oblivion,
I silently sat, pondering,
staring at him and at me—wondering.
I was engulfed by darkness,
dreaming of a caravan that would pass by
and pull me out of my deep well.
He was out there,
brandishing his gun in full sight,
making his monotonous patrol,
over the high fence.
"You hardly know me!" I said—
and I barely know you,
not even your first name.
Had our steps ever crossed in the souk's chatter and clatter,
as you roamed your two empty shells over shop façades,
we would have considered each other
an anonymous figure.
Then how on earth could we become enemies?
Are we truly so?
Isn't he who is right here,
keeping both of us restlessly sleepless,
a drop after drop draining us out of peaceful slumber,
the same one who is sound asleep down there!?
Isn't he who is tonight pitting us against each other,
splitting us into two opposites,
the same one who will, tomorrow,
fuse us back as a perfect twin,
united by tormenting pain—

when the earth is shaken to her utmost convulsion,
and throws up her burdens from within,
and rage storms through the morning's veins—
Then how come our sole line of communication,
should be this deadly piece?"
I said to him,
. . . .
. . . .

But he briefly squinted his two empty shells,
then aimed his nostrils up at the air,
and went about,
like a cold-stricken, puffing warm air onto his emaciated, chilly limbs.

The Pre-Eruption Silence

AALIM ABBAS

Calm now,
but a storm in disguise!
Calm now,
but a bomb masked in silence,
boiling with wrath,
though cool and collected on the surface.
A calm:
discreetly assembling its rage atoms,
setting orbit for its imminent upheaval,
for the sweeping waves of its rampant masses.
A calm:
building up its rampage, clenching its fist,
tuning its vocal chords for the victory songs.
A calm:
composing verse in praise of its auspicious procession;
deploying its ranks and files,
for the final showdown.
A calm:
amassing thunder and lightning,
to bandage its bleeding veins.
A calm:
for us to fill our eyes of the killer's bleeding knife.
A calm:
for us to prod the horses,
with the spur of the impending uprising.
A calm:
to silence rumor mongers,
and lay bare plots of double-dealers,
in the glow of its exposing flames.
A calm:

outwitting the double-minded,
uncovering the mean games of dirty agents
and the lies of the fake-faced, bearded crooks.
A calm:
reminiscent of death serenity,
yet it is the lull before the storm.
Let those shaky souls never feel safe.
Let the flame of protest inside us never fade away.
Let the scary eyes never nod out.
Alas!
The night's silence lulls to sleep the heart-free poets,
but their notebooks remain wakeful and alert,
and their verse—trapped in their pens—
oozing with revolt;
and their inkpots revving with fury.
Let revolt in the veins boil with fume;
Let it never subside.
Until peace reined,
until justice was made.
Let no criminal get away with it.
Let the judges lose nothing of their resolve and fairness.
A calm,
setting its course,
to shake the tyrants' crowns, devastate their strongholds,
force them out of their hideouts.
A calm, like a furious volcano,
coming out of a deep nap,
to tell everyone,
that tyranny is a big lie,
that blood is innocent and sacred.

The Homesick Sparrow

MAHJOUB SHARIF

A homesick sparrow
perches on the heart's window.
With longing eyes,
it cranes out to glance at the houses,
at the distant skies,
waiting for a cheerful morning,
with promises laden,
to land like a turban,
on the shoulder of the homeland.
With each coup in a dark abyss we plunge.
The heavy-footed junta besiege our songs.
They agitate our inkpot, confiscate its internal peace.
They poison the cheerful spring
and place their muzzles on everything.
What a pleasant dream they disfigure,
in the eyes of each mother.
But they can't manage to silence us. Never.
In their cells we sip,
the perseverance syrup,
to remain bold and steadfast.
O my times in incarceration.
O my pain of longing and torment.
If I lose touch with you,
who, in this time of coercion, would I be?
If I lose touch with you I will betray
the little ones yet to come.
If I lose touch with you,
conceited and self-centered I will become.
So long as I have a voice in my chords,
what prison—or even death—can silence me?

No. We will never succumb.
They have no say
in our destiny. No they don't.
We are the ones who bring life
to the dead pores of dormancy.
O my sweetheart,
my life partner,
in high regards I will always keep you.
O my beloved daughters,
nestled in the shade of kind people.
O the luminous space in the eye range:
warm me up with your peaceful greetings,
with your letters.
Give my greetings to my peers.
Give my greetings to the clouds.
Give my greetings to the earth.
Give my greetings to the crowds
and to the words of romance,
in the notebooks of schoolchildren.

Crazy in Love with You

MAHJOUB SHARIF

I'm crazy in love with you.
You've taken up the depth of my soul for a home
and my pulse as your standing guard.
In your warmth I live,
the loveliest episode of my life.
In your abode I find my best resort.
And along the shores of your eyes
my favorite stroll.
In your company,
my life starts to become meaningful,
and no door is closed any more.
I see the world as a fascinating mound,
the morning breeze spreading its pillows around.
Thanks to you, the river and I
become intimate friends,
and my eyes fall in love,
with the cheeks of the flower.
I'm again on excellent terms with me,
and my chronic wounds heal.
Back on my feet,
I call out your name;
to its rhythm I dance and sing.
And I defiantly proclaim:
Your warmth has brought me back to life.
You've made up for my times of sorrow,
times of torment and strife.
And when our eyes met,
I came to embrace the soft rain of joy I'd long missed.
I wish we'd crossed paths earlier.
I wish we'd met a little earlier.

I Say It without Fear

MAHJOUB SHARIF

I say it without fear:
I'm not afraid to die,
never bother when,
how,
or where.
Watching the stars in a summer night.
A bullet in the heart.
A deadly stab.
I'm not afraid to die,
never bother when,
how,
or where.
In a dark spot.
In a crowd.
Or on the road.
I'm not afraid to die,
in a fire.
And drowning is not dreadful either.
I surely don't fear dying in bed,
with my wife,
two daughters,
neighbors,
relatives,
friends,
my cat,
my lovely hut,
and my water jar—
all around.
Well-groomed, I proceed,
neatly dressed in white I lead

the grand procession to my eternal abode.
Of death I have no fear,
in any form it may appear.
What I do fear, though,
what makes me particularly anxious,
is death dealing a blow,
to my conscience.

Buffoon!

MAHJOUB SHARIF

Hey, buffoon!
hold on tight, buffoon!
lest you fall down.
Crack down on the stubborn.
Snoop around.
Beware. Of everything beware,
of your own shadow.
Never feel shy.
If the tree leaves rustle,
quickly take shelter.
Walking around is not without danger.
Stop it.
Shoot at everything,
at every gust of wind—without warning,
at every word traveling without passport.
Train each bird to file an intelligence report.
Train all windows in cities,
all lanterns in villages,
all stems of sorghum.
Have all ants join the informants ranks.
Have the drizzle write intelligence reports.
Even better, pack all the people in bottles.
Keep a close watch on the starving.
Stamp the hell out of the downtrodden,
shell and bomb them down.
Confiscate the stars from the night,
the tide from the sea.
Scratch the morning face.
Cut down the wind's wings.
Block life's veins

and send hope to exile;
hope brought in
by the discovery of fire
and division of labor.
Perhaps then
you can get a safe haven,
Buffoon!

The Golden Scythe Song

MAHGOUB KBALO

The flowers on your skirts,
are courting the park flowers,
across the creek.
I won't send you flowers.
I know you won't forgive plucking them.
The lure of your prancing,
keeps all sins away from our embrace heaven.
The guard who said he saw us behind the night veil,
running over hills of slumber,
will never have sore eyes, I assure you.
Just as the downpour can expose my missing seeds,
your tears can unearth my lost flowers.
"How come we parted?" your innocent question,
forgetting our earthly origin,
and the four seasons' sway over us.
All the instruments of romance are present:
the grove,
the fountain,
and the silence carved by your whispers.
When I met you
I realized all the world cities are females.
You are the Babylon of all cities.
Come closer.
One step farther and I'm burned down to ashes.
Your silk-soft voice hits my patience as a lion's roar.
You are my fifth season, sweetheart.
When beads roll down the space between my skin and clothes.
You recoil from the trap of my mail,
I long for the life vest of your reply.
Your silence shuts me off.

Talk to me,
And I'll win the intrigue of another jasmine.

I come to life on two occasions:
when you set in my heart,
and when you rise on my soul's horizon.
The henna paint on your feet is a shade
from Queen Bilqis's palace.
Strolling on musk soil is made for you.
Your smile, sweetheart,
beams like fingers of an orange sun
waking up a time in slumber.
Like seasoned wine in the king's stock,
your kisses expose:
forts
lakes
soldiers
arms
nets
and countless stuff.
You dismount a bridal cart,
carried by the white swans of my litanies,
to the apex of my longing for you.
In transit between exposure and veil,
deep in the bush,
you look like a crescent tripping over the clouds.
When your sofa finally took us in,
I became certain of King Solomon's death,
because all his treasures were in your possession.

Deng Malo

A Biography   MAHGOUB KBALO

A name cast from clay:
Deng Malo.
From the bike age.
Under a hat the hollow color of a Tuesday, the color of a desolate
    printing press,
and a coat made of guffaws.
His abode is this song.
His bed the bare ground—history's eldest bed.
His cover the posters of a cinema movie,
with heavy rain scenes.
His snoring decorates the song with the route of a dusting plane roaming
    the morning sky.
His dream is of girls the color of his girlfriend,
before colors spoilt the beauty of cinema.
When the sun stings him
he jumps from his bed onto his wire dog: the bike,
singing out loud:
If I owned a hill of bread,
a lake of stew,
and a bush of *tunbak* snuff,
I would love you,
even if you were a different woman.

Pastoral Scriptures

MAHGOUB KBALO

The sun opened the cloud's window,
and dried the shirt I'm wearing to the date.
"Nails are windows," said the green manicure.
"The body is a fort," said the abyss,
between your breasts and the sea level.
I spend the whole night,
setting traps for the mice
that devour our larvae.
Your steps flicker across the brasiliensis trees and the breeze.
I screen the passageway
but can't see you rolling down.
My small heaven sets me ablaze.
I was on my way to you,
in full bloom, chased by butterflies,
elegant, like the Satan who introduced football to the world.
The water master was neatly dressed:
a sky-blue jacket
a red handkerchief
a moss rod
and a slumber cap.
In a remote corner,
an invisible ironsmith
was fixing the drainage gutters
and offering for sale
chewing gum, cigarettes,
and many items the soul's color.
Though a Sunday,
it was the only day that continued
to bleed flowers onto the year's diary.
Our moon was high that night.

Having galloped a Sudanese half-noon,
it coronated cretaceous dervishes as Bonapartes and Führers.
and sent us to exile, barefooted.
We were demolishing bridges leading to heavens,
coloring time's fluff with our lips,
and watching passing towers in your washing water.
Then we cautiously went out
to capture live twilights,
disguised in lizards' attires,
and cast our nets on mollusks tucked to the music bottom.
You teach me how to pronounce your name;
I teach you my pastoral alphabets,
engraved on my quicklime,
over it my goats' shoes afloat
behind the crosses of my grass.
I drive my barefooted goats,
treading the steps of your kids
to the boundaries of the galaxy,
near your eyelids.
At your glance,
I become full of colors like a schoolteacher.
Full of picnic
pastor
raving
sacred
assigned with washing urchins
and drying up the cooing.
When you close your eyes,
I fly off your windows.
A demon of dust,
in your absence, full of lust,
landing on the beds of low height homes.

The Silent Rose

FIDAILI JAMMA'

My rose is besieged in fear.
I tiptoe to climb her silence.
Holding my breath:
I know, my rose,
you are waiting for the first threads of light
to gracefully come out
of the blind darkness,
for the sunrays,
for a soft shower to wash dryness
off the heads of trees and huts
and quench earth's thirst,
after a long, scorching summer.
As though, with your heart's eyes,
our Zarqaa of Yamama,[1]
you can see a time ahead,
when the grass comes out dancing,
to the rhythm of the storming streets.
With your heart's eyes,
you can see millet fields in full bloom,
the air filled with peasants' guffaws,
and breasts heavy with milk,
and a pleasant morning breeze
after a long night of hunger,
and your fragrance regaining dominance over the air,
despite the beleaguering fear.
In your silence the big secret lies,
and behind the eloquent silence,
the once dominant fear
is given a humiliating defeat.
In silence it does retreat!

A Sun on the Window

FIDAILI JAMMA'

The pleasant morning sun landed on my window.
Imprinted a kiss full of flowers and rubies,
then away she flew.
Through the window of my heart
I saw my homeland
and heard the echo of your whispering words.
A stream, washed by the rains of my homeland!
I saw the banks of the green paradise
in my mother's smile!
and our ultimate hopes,
in the giggles of our young ones.
I rose up, breathless, singing—
but couldn't see the sunrays,
or your whispering words,
or my mother's smile.
They've stolen the sun
and gathered around me!
Yet in the rapture of my dreams,
I found myself transformed into a homeland
carrying through airports and checkpoints
my past,
my future,
and my dreams;
my love stories, and the sleepless nights,
my mother,
and the tales of my beloved homeland.

Walking a Tightrope

FIDAILI JAMMA'

We are no longer a chess pawn;
no matter how strong you may have grown.
We've learnt how to break the strongest of arms.
We dare to smash the dragon's eggs
and gouge out the cyclops's eye.
We've learnt how to sing out to our heart's content,
to transform the night's sorrows to rhymes
and fill the sky with pleasant melodies.
We've learnt how to walk a tightrope
and pass through a needle's eye,
defeating the pain living inside us
and dig a grave for you.
You wish you could detain
the street protestors' chants
and arrest those roaring waves
and this pleasant dawn about to break.
Taking shelter behind your gun trigger,
in panic from head to toes you shiver,
from the thunderstorms bolting out of our throats.
You peek your eyes,
counting the pulse rising from the street asphalt
from the roaring waves
from our chants
echoing the bitterness of your heinous acts.
Here we are, resisting our misery.
We shall resist your troops,
fend off the froth of your lies
all the pettinesses of your time.
We shall resist your shade.

We shall challenge fear and break the dragon's eggs
and gouge out the cyclops's eye.
We shall embrace the emerging dawn,
studded with our sons' blood,
emerging from the heart of darkness.

The Shores of Your Eyes

A glimpse of you!
"Ah! The shore!" I scream.
And I lose myself to dream.
I pull myself together,
and with the power still left in me,
I pull hard on the oars.
Your eyes looming ahead:
Shores shimmering in the horizon.
Your smile rising high: a beacon.
And I lose myself to dream.
The fiercer the wind grows,
diverting the waves,
the more stubborn I become.
I swear by your name,
to reverse the course of the stream.
You are the port I'm bound for,
unless I drown in transit.
Worries beset me, though,
that my heavy cloud of dreams
might go astray with the wind
and disperse away.
Full of fears and worries I grow.
I pull hard on the oars,
and with the power still left in me,
I reach to you,
a wrecked soul, calamity-scarred,
a grief-stricken heart.
I come down to you.
My strings tautened,
I relate the tale of a man,

who took a permanent abode along your course,
marked his senses with your face,
pulled hard on the oars,
and solemnly declared,
You are the port I'm bound for,
unless I drown in transit.
Fears beset me, though.
Full of fear I grow
that the shore might take you in its folds and retreat
before I hit land;
that all my heavy clouds of dreams
might go astray with the wind
and disperse away.

I Miss Something

ABDULQADIR ALKUTAYABI

*Perhaps it is sudden waking from a sober slumber! No! It's engrossment in
the depth of engrossment! No, it's rather a vision I drifted into out of the
corridors of another vision. No, no. It's splinters of ruins in the collisions of
mirrors where the joints of the truth were smashed.*

I feel I'm missing something I can't afford to lose . . .
Not my grandfather; not my father.
Something alive has parted me.
Not my eyes.
Not my hands either.
Not my soul, not my own self.
Something that has left a cold spot in my memory.
Have I lost (the grand secret) in my inner being?
I am afraid I am slipping away from me.
My greatest fear is fear per se.
Here I am, hallucinating—missing something;
something serious that I can't recall.
I wonder how I can pass by the idol
and not smash it.
I ask myself:
How can I love God with this heart,
and with the very same heart I fall in love
with someone who disbelieves in Him?
How come, I ask myself, I feel tired from crossing
the span between the heart's sidewalk,
And my tongue's root?!
I feel the caravan I'm in is not mine.
I'm crossing a time not mine!
Not mine!
Not mine! It's a nightmare.

Confused dreams—endless episodes of injustice—darkness.
I ask myself—Why should I ask her?!
I truly feel I'm missing something I can't afford to lose.
Not a woman; not a sip or a bite.
I feel like a pole whose flag and cause
have flown away.
I feel like the two edges of a sword,
that desperately misses both the leader and the mission.

Uncle Abdur Raheem

MOHAMMED EL-HASSAN SALIM HIMMAID

"My omniscient, bountiful Lord,"
he intoned, summing up his dawn prayers
in hums and whispers.
His string of beads shaking feverishly in his fingers,
invoking divine blessings on the loved ones.
Bowing his head,
worries tumbled down—sticky and dense.
Looking up,
it was a barren sky,
save for a thin streak of clouds
and some shy distant stars—
it was summer time.
She wasn't there to say "Good morning"
or ask if he slept well.
No intimate touch,
an affectionate gesture,
from a warm heart,
like the old days,
the good, old days.
No, she was not in.
She was in the pen,
saddling his donkey,
and milking the goats
for the morning tea.
Before the birds had ruffled up their feathers
and begun their dawn twitter,
Uncle Abdur Raheem dragged himself out.
Down at the shore, he met with partners in strife—
from all corners they descended:
from Jeraif,

and from Jebel.
"Hope everyone is well,"
he bantered with them.
They teased him—he damned them.
No hard feelings, though—
For Uncle Abdur Raheem holds no grudges,
no one here does—
Grudge against who?
They are all friends,
they are all relatives,
bonded together, if not by blood,
then surely by trade and occupation,
by aspiration and frustration too.
"Cheer up, fellow,
keep the hope alive.
Never feel low.
Tomorrow will be better.
On hard work and hope we shall thrive."
Uncle Abdur-Raheem:
As a farmer, you were your own master,
free to sleep,
free to get up at leisure—
no attendance sheets,
no clocking in,
no meal breaks, fixed and tight,
Free to water your land in moonlight
and plough under the stars.
But time is a wheel in a perpetual spin.
On his ride to work,
the *tukul* rose high on his screen,
and old wounds came alive.
If only he could wipe them clean!
in a twinkling!
Each dawn, his day begins from the tukul.

There they sit, dwelling on issues,
chronic and stubborn each day they grow,
too hard to tackle:
money for lunch,
the school uniform,
a debt long overdue.
In the midst of this gloom, though,
faint glimpses of hope linger,
from afar they flicker.
That morning, Ammoona finally spoke out:
"The shoes and the tobe are worn out."
She didn't demand money, though.
"Don't worry, sweetheart.
Just drop them,
to the nearby cobbler and tailor."
"How come—Om al-Hassan?
They won't stand a single stitch!
Only worse they can get!
You've got to have a new tobe—
at any cost,
no matter what.
So—Om Rahoum—you shouldn't feel down,
when you go out with neighbors,
to a wedding,
or to congratulate a neighbor,
on a good score by a brilliant son or daughter—
it's the least you should do.
Life is worthless except in a shared moment of celebration or sympathy.
Uncle Abdur Raheem,
are you really a free man?
"If only the date palms were to bear more often!
If only the old good days hadn't passed
like a dream!
You wouldn't have been humiliated,

Om Rahoum,
or met any harm.
You wouldn't have stifled with dismay,
or sunk in despair, and dearth—
And I would have showered you with precious gifts.
Governments out, to oblivion.
Governments in, over us they reign—
with fairy tales and illusion,
fallacies and game,
being their sacred constitution.
At times, the military's bullying hands,
at others, the graveyards,
ruling us in the Prophet's name.
Sometimes you bristle.
Sometimes you give in, make no fuss.
Sometimes you join drumbeaters,
and sycophantic entourage.
It's time to stand up, boy.
It's time to wipe your eyes clear of the mirage.
How many cycles you have to endure—
like a patient soil?
All the seeds you had sown died.
You have nothing left but a few date palms.
Your land lay fallow,
no new seeds to sow,
no pump on the run,
and the salary is a bubble.
Spit on you!
miserable of a world!
Spit on you!
Despite your constant grief,
O poor man,
you never complained,
despite stifling miseries,

and hardships weighing heavily upon you,
and market demons,
having a free rein,
driving you in a perpetual marathon,
cruel and insane.
But you are by no means alone,
in your sorrow,
Uncle Abdur Raheem,
there are others no less unfortunate,
living in rented dwelling.
No land, no palm trees of their own.
And others who can't afford even a burrow,
trading their muscle strength and sweat for a scanty living:
the sun-scorched,
city workers,
porters,
sailors,
cane cutters,
cotton pickers,
rope hawkers,
bakers: fused by oven flames
and a blazing weather.
What a life!
for the debt-ridden,
like a cart horse,
working daylong, for pennies,
sometimes for less,
look how much they get?
and how many mouths on their feed list?
And here are the well-heeled:
clusters of factories,
farmsteads—expansive swathes,
no worries,
no beads of sweat on foreheads,

no frowns on faces.
Little these fortunes weigh, be assured,
against the eternal bliss of paradise—
and heavenly mansions.
But these are way beyond reach now, Abdur-Raheem—
A grave stands in transit, in between.
He chirrups his donkey.
Don't give free rein,
to your mind's eye.
Surely, Abdur-Raheem,
poverty whittles away faith,
from the boldest of hearts.
The time spin wheel tosses governments out, to oblivion,
and others onto the reign,
governing us with fairy tales and illusion,
with fallacies and game,
being their sacred constitution,
at times, with the military's bullying hands,
at others, the graveyards,
ruling us in the Prophet's name.
Sometimes you bristle,
sometimes you give in, make no fuss,
sometimes you join,
the drumbeaters,
and sycophantic entourage.
It's time to stand up, boy.
It's time to stand the course!
You have had enough.
It's time to wipe your eyes clear of the mirage.
All the seeds you had sown died.
You have nothing left but the date palms.
Your land lay fallow,
no new seeds,
no pump on the run.

He chirrups the donkey,
his nudge on the beast's belly
triggers his own memory:
"Don't forget the sandal,
the tobe, the noon meal,
the school uniform,
the travel permit,
for the son heading south,
to join the army—
And his mind went on full spin,
like an ignited torch:
a son unwilling to re-sit
the exam, but unable to get
a job either,
cores of prejudice,
a daughter deserted by her groom,
destitution, drought,
and relief remains as elusive and beyond reach as ever.
We've never seen a situation as worse, never—
And his mind went on full spin.
The railway crossing . . .
Watch the traiiiin, uncle!
The traiiin—Watch out, Abdur Raheem!—
a blood stream
And gushing tears.
And only fate was there to blame.
Though eyewitnesses did see the blood stream,
and gushing tears.
Their hands on the earth,
their eyes on the train,
they know the bottom truth.
And the news spread,
from the mouths of children,
and city workers,

it passed to flying birds,
was picked up by the sea waves,
and heavy clouds:
Uncle Abdur Raheem,
on his drive along the road,
tilted leftward,
to evade a patrol wagon.
As if seeing a dragon,
his startled donkey plunged down,
like a heavy stone,
casting off its load,
and Uncle Abdur Raheem,
hit the train head-on.
So on that dawn,
a stream of blood, chunky with sun-baked earth,
flew down,
and spilled onto:
a circular,
a medical prescription,
a posted letter,
the pay for the month,
two overtime slips—
scattered around a saddle pad,
with a broken back.

Uncle Abdur Raheem,
how many souls are taking refuge in you?
So shed off this false shroud,
wake them all up,
to your serene, eternal world.
Uncle Abdur Raheem,
how many souls are taking refuge in you?
So shed off this false shroud,
wake them all up,
to your serene, eternal world.

Nura and the Time-Tested Dream

MOHAMMED EL-HASSAN SALIM HIMMAID

Hey girls!
Wait!
Is Nura with you?
Nura . . .
The hard-working farmer,
who milks the goats,
for the young ones and guests.
When it turns to a blaze,
Nura turns to a breeze;
making the rounds,
offering the starving a bite,
the thirsty a sip;
and on the sleepless,
alone in the darkness,
she does tenderly lean,
soothing their pain,
lending them a smile for tomorrow.
For the bare-skinned she brings new wear,
though her own gown is a threadbare.
Haven't you seen her?
You don't know what you missed.
Nura . . . the earth child,
my beloved sister,
sister of all the downtrodden,
a shield against misfortune—
and for those who lose their way a beacon.
From the heart of the bountiful soil she sprouted.
The heavy cloud we've long longed for.
Now the Lord has brought her to us.
The Lord has brought her to us.

A drum in the south,
lulling the woes of the dog-tired;
a *tambur*[1] in the north,
wiping the tears of the gloom-engulfed.
If you don't know her,
then you don't know what you missed.
Nura thought she should learn how to read
but the world's heavy wall against her leaned.
She put the book aside,
picked up her scythe,
and back and forth she ran,
cutting and mowing.
In her brisk jerks,
she hurt her hand.
She picked some earth
and sprinkled it on the wound.
Once at the *donka*,[2] she was bitten;
at night came the *fekki*[3] and made some spells.
Another day, cramps swept her body.
Came the *baseer*[4] and cauterized her.
She never dared groan
or ask those around to leave her alone.
Once she saw in a dream,
a bird eating her own chick,
a wall standing on its tiptoes,
hurling stones at its builder's back.
At Seedi's estate,
she heard a young palm sapling,
fervently telling the crowd behind her:
this land is destined to fall back
into the hands of those who long ploughed it.
She saw the Nile waves jumping and cheering,
She was thirsty, her lips descaled and dry.
The sun called off her forenoon.

All creatures met with their creator.
She saw a fire,
remnants of a human
on the chopping log of a labyrinth
a divine light,
like a mirage glimmering,
tied with her to the night's wedge,
at some point,
between the city and the bewilderment—
She explained her dream to them.
She must have gone mad, they thought,
adding to her misery.
Back to the fields,
she started anew,
cutting and mowing,
building nests for birds,
finding solace in waterwheels,
when they gush out their longing: *oshshsh*!
She started anew
watering, planting,
running around, making tools
working day through night.
She endured misery,
but she never endured cheating!
With forbearance by the Lord endowed,
and vigor from the land gained,
all day she works hard.
When the night falls,
she goes in and waters her tiny plot,
to quench her plants' thirst,
and feed her young ones.
Back at home,
the dreams of the poor,
bleed out of her confused eyes.

Off she sweeps dust of misfortune,
and implants long-cherished wishes.
Sleepless, she then sits, dreaming
of houses with power and shower
of love overflowing in the streets
filling all hearts.
Nura dreams of a life
free of all strains
and a homeland
that knows no fences or chains,
of worlds
as dreamy as children's visions:
no hassles,
no woes or military coups,
no aggrieved or grieves.
Nura dreams
and when she dreams,
Nura shrieks,
and when she shrieks,
Nura dreams.
And when the wind of the bitter reality
blows off her tiny nest of dreams,
Nura bleeds;
and her inner self chants:
justice will reign one day,
justice will reign one day,
justice will reign one day.
Once again Nura starts to dream,
when she dreams,
Nura shrieks.
and when she shrieks,
Nura dreams,
she daydreams,
true daydreams.

The Story of a Revolution

HASHIM SIDDIG

As the prolonged night of tyranny showed no signs of fading,
and no dawn was on the horizon,
we decided to stand up and recall the glory of our ancestors
who defeated the aggressors,
and tore down their strongholds.
One night, our masses were out grappling,
with barricades of all sorts.
A strong chant came from down the street:
We will never succumb, we swear
for freedom-aspirants revolution is the way.
And the street boiled with revolt;
like a flame, rage flew past,
we defeated the dark night. Yes we did.
Light finally found its way home,
and dignity found its way to the hearts of the free people.
My beloved homeland: we are the swords of your glory.
Our parades will always be on alert to protect your soil.
The streets have seen how on the day of rage we poured out,
to aromatize the revolution's field with our blood
in sacrifice of our homeland's freedom.
In October, the dawn of the storm,
we broke down the stubborn chains of the past
when our parades fumed out.
Steadfast, boiling, storming, and chanting:
Bullets cannot defeat us.
Blood streams ran across the valley.
We offered our lives in sacrifice,
to bring back light to you, my beloved homeland.
It was a saga the whole world stood watching in awe.
And the pleasant dawn of October broke again on our land.

It all began at the university;
an angry demonstration was out roaring,
determined to wipe out the gloomy darkness.
But the gloomy darkness responded with venom and smoke,
and the whole Sudan woke up to the sound of bullets.
The angry masses poured out,
determined to force out the long-lasting darkness.
Gorashi was our first in martyr,
but we didn't back off.
We swore to withhold and resist the stifling darkness.
We offered our lives in sacrifice and stayed the course.
We pledged to force our way to light, or die in transit.
Each step, we came across a martyr,
with their blood a sketch of the victory dawn is drawn.
You know, dear October,
we have endured countless nights,
in chains, torment, and humiliation.
Our chests raging like a volcano,
we pledged to write Sudan's name in the book of glory.
Our blood streamed out, filled the square,
but we swore to press ahead.
We brandished the swords of civil obedience.
Hand in hand, we pledged to stand in resistance.
No backing off, no compromise.
We had an account to settle with you, tyrant.
Our steps were on the road to victory.
Our roaring chants rocking the palace walls.
We demolished barricades, removed barriers.
In one line we stood:
workers, students, peasants, artisans.
We defeated the dark night. Yes we did.
And light finally found its way home,
and dignity found its way to the hearts of the free people.
Oh the Palace Square, a field of fire,

an oasis embracing the soul of Nassar.
We've fed your flowers with revolutionary blood,
implanted your space with the chanting of freedom fighters,
decorated your soil with luminous words
telling the story of our revolt days.
Our martyrs on our shoulders, we marched, chanting,
the burning wounds in our hearts oozing.
We laid our martyrs to rest
and rushed back to continue resistance.
No backing off. No compromise.
Then suddenly, as we stood there,
our ranks closed and tight,
the revolution dawn finally broke
like a dream that came true,
and light found its way home at last,
and dignity found its way to the hearts of the free people.
Take this pledge from us, October:
We will protect your slogan.
We will nurture your tree.
We will raise the treasured revolution's flag
high at full mast
embroidered with the revolution's slogan,
bright and evergreen.
And here is one more pledge for you, October:
Whenever a tyrant raids on us at dawn,
we will stand up in resistance and fight.
We will protect the revolution's slogan.
Endless columns lined up, chanting
till the dreamy dawn is back again.

The Tale of the Rose and the Street

HASHIM SIDDIG

Prologue:
To the rose I bowed,
not to the wind,
or the caliph's sword.
To a genuine smile I bowed,
to a warbling tear,
and a tasty bite,
to relief, in the comfort of a loaf of bread.
To a moon sticking his tongue out
at the awful darkness;
I did a bow,
to a wound braving its pain;
to a nation,
above narrow interests rising;
to a morning,
with intimately rosy features;
to a heart,
green and forgiving.
I bowed to shake hands,
with clean hands.
A perfect bow is due,
to the streets;
to a homeland,
beloved and proud;
to a hope,
from my wounds sprouting;
to a pen,
not for sale;
to eyes,
vigilant and noble

I did a bow,
to huts,
harbors,
exile shelters,
waterwheels,
to live coal in harsh winter,
to words,
patient and chaste.
I did a bow,
to my people: the beacon,
to the handkerchiefs,
the wheat spikes
the folksongs
to impudence
to hearts: bold and tender.
To the rose I bowed,
not to the wind,
or the caliph's sword.

A Starting Point

AZHARI MOHAMMED ALI

Which point shall I start you from—
When I still hold some of your fear and grief?
Where shall I start you from—
When in my belief,
you inspired the birth of life, inspired life to come to life,
and caused setbacks and ordeals to demise?
I wish I can find you,
so my total self would become part of you;
or so part of me would become part of your total self.
I long to be you,
and unite our divided blood circle and complexion.
Where shall I start you from?
From me?
From you, inch by inch?
Which entry point shall I enter you through—
When all entrances are blocked by bees?
Which road leads to you—
When all the routes are soaked in mud?
I beat all barriers and get in,
through your utterance I enter you;
through your pores.
Through each common factor,
and any remote resemblance I enter you,
and we meet!
Two rivers
of subliming and longing.
And I start you
from where the ends of the end ended at your end.
I start you,
and I pluck out the tents of my past years

to find your hands all stretched,
your contention doors wide open.
I start you from the moment I was attracted to your fire
and took direction from your firebrand.
None of the routes that cannot get to you,
or relay some of your echo,
will ever lure me.
Where shall I start you from?

Songs of Solitude

AL-SADDIG AL-RADDI

Just as thin light slips away
onto the sea surface,
loaded with the fragrance
of a prophet moon,
the essence of magic,
chants of the ultimate joy,
and the murmur of elements in the deep structure of light—
souls ascend on the back of waves,
intoning silver as part of water's features,
a thread of foam smoke in the flute's whisper,
and the hums on the lips of houris,
swimming freely between the depth and the surface,
the space of a seashell-like awe,
colorlessness,
where silence is the gate to the internal existence
of the sea kingdom and the aqueous code.
Take a window from the sunrays,
and soar into the skies of absence,
to an eternal departure.
You have no place herein now.
And God dwells everywhere:
a face glittering across alleyways,
a street leading to the bread—the unattainable food,
and as far as the wear of the poor—
Oh, what is there looming out of the windows?
A lover's scarf, the color of the sea?
Hot tears spilling on the bosom of a lonely lover?
The taste of fire?
And the birds, the consummation of dew,
in the dream's terrace,

packing the horizon,
searching for their childhood in the memory of the open space,
and the dawn canned in the shelves of silence,
and songs' invisible jargon hiding within the pores of grass,
and the trees disguised in tree statues.
Grief wouldn't choose to dress in tears,
just to be named "crying."
It's something that comes out of soul's splinters,
traverses the grand blood fountains,
and sneaks away through the border of the black material;
something that never dissolves within the beaches of color
and never looks like a gelatinous substance in the zones of nothingness.
The grief inside ourselves is more of a walking being,
within us strolling in two legs,
a circled object orbiting the universe,
deleting from the rays of silence the lasting memory of tranquility.
How can braids explode into silver in light,
and the bubbles between the drizzle woman,
into a signal to the wind in the vigorous rain,
a light in water,
a thread of dew droplets
charm . . .
prayers . . .
altar . . .
twilight?
That's the secret of the universe:
to see in each beauty,
a sign of the Lord,
a glimpse of His Kingdom,
And that imposing divine charm.
That's the secret of justice:
things gushing out,
laying bare their holiness.
The probable becoming certain,

then treasures open up.
The land has been hoarding wheat stocks
for her children,
so poor they use earth for pillows.
Tell those who in the name of the Lord
are dispensing injustice on the streets:
the Lord is there, in the fire of tears
in the bread queues!
in the carts and the marketplace!
in the devastated rooms!
Oh the sea . . . the voice of mother-ladies
Oh the draft . . . the silence of "mother-men"
God is alive, immortal . . . everlasting . . .
How come the once stinking, fetid air
is now a pleasantly aromatic odor?
A wind building up the grand ingredients of the street;
a scent: an antidote of that stench.
History is repeating itself!
Gone are all those lovely songs we chanted by Nile Street,
in the fold of waves taken,
plunged to oblivion
swept away, as all but a wreckage in the beaches
or feed for seaweeds.
A sound sliding into the bottom
in the reining silence over remote distances.
We are now in the time of great grief,
the moment of great calamity,
emotional vacuum,
we will cry no more, now!
But who will dare trade this for the days to come?
What are we going to lose?
In our exile, we carve out,
a land that sees nothing in the mirror
but her own image;

a woman: a language made of ashes
who betrays her lover in defiance of daylight.
Never trust your heart; love is futile.
More worthwhile is pushing through silence,
through the inner self;
awareness of coming to being
and the individual being transformed into
a total equal to the infinite power,
locating things by referring to them in name,
frittering the gelatin,
penetrating the strongholds of secrecy,
opening up the windows of things,
highlighting tiny details,
a power that blows up dreams and memories,
the false lovers—dummies, and friends.
Never trust your heart: so light can ascend and inundate all spaces;
peer around,
pick up your place and burn yourself up just there!
Now you are the blood gauge,
the blaze—the fire,
the rage stove.
You are, hence, the moment's glare to come.
I, you, we, the people
the street
those poles extending along the asphalt
my voice/your voice: ruptured
in the decayed seats and collapsing parliament.
I didn't say: scandal has erupted flickering,
from the folds of the turban,
and the stretch of the false beard.
Why didn't you say,
that the buildings grew up taller and taller,
and spewed your hungry children
onto the filthy sidewalks?

You know they stand against you,
against us,
against me.
And I know I will always remain against the power—the unconsciousness.
Now we are at the heart of the cause,
the heart of the fire,
and there at the peripheries, the power of the deep language prevails,
light enough to stick to the hollowness.
Yes. We will forget all what they do and say.
We will nail them down—
naked against history's gate,
then fill up the days in the mythical, horrific silence.
You are made not of light to forgive,
but of clay to build.
So build a house for me . . .
for us . . .
for you . . .
for the coming ones.
If justice really exists on earth,
so let our blood be the gauge.
If heaven stands versus to earth,
so let blood be versus to earth
The Lord said: Be . . .
and we did.
But have we ascertained the existence of the matter in our inner souls
against Genesis and creation?
We come out of the confines of grand isolation
only to write about the songs of grand isolation
but we are soon hit by grief as we come out,
inside silence,
and in the heart of the question.

Heart's Confessions

RAWDA EL-HAJ

Every day I get more convinced
that I was created for you alone.
It is through your eyes that I saw the world;
on your lips my poems were born.
Without you,
my life is a wasteland.
I am colorless,
tasteless,
smelling like a land never visited by rain.
Every day I get more convinced
that I am a matchstick.
Only once it can ignite,
so be the one who lights me
and let me illuminate your fields at night.
No one but you knows the secret
of keeping my match alive
for long years to come—a full life.
No one but you
can lend life a beautiful color.
No one but you
can convince my heart,
the stubborn, skeptic heart of mine
to break the bad habit
of breaking away.
Every day I get more convinced
that it would be a bluff to say
your presence was not the strongest tremor
my monitors have ever registered.
Calling you "buddy,"
or "part" of me,

or a small symbol adorning my verse
is just not accurate.
Obeying my female intuition,
I conceal our affair even from my closest friends,
but your lovely voice comes out in spite of me.
Your jasmine scent inundates my solemn vocabulary
and my vocabulary exposes me—
What a shame!
My secret perfume comes out in public!
How can I run away from my own conviction,
which is besieging me like a fence of grass and jasmine?
Every day I get more convinced;
for God's sake, give me more conviction!

A New Ebb in the High Tide Season

RAWDA EL-HAJ

I surely can't take it anymore.
This heart of mine is full of holes, wounds, and defeat.
My endurance waned.
My grief swelled to a mount.
All wounds exposed their legs.
It's revealing time;
so come forth, my wounds, and show off,
and let the tears tell the how, what, and if.
I have long shunned you,
but here you came now,
at the peak of fear!
I concealed my heartbeats,
resisted all temptations,
but soon caved in.
Then I backed off again
and banned your face from entering my city,
posted your portraits in all inlets and ports,
but it nevertheless kept appearing,
in the households,
in the faces
and the flashes of eyes.
If you knew
how much I suffered from wounds, old and new,
you might show mercy on me.
If you knew,
how I peeked for smiles
from the faces of comers and goers,
how I struggled to bring myself to balance
in order to afford a laugh when I meet you.
If you knew,

how I shelved sorrows,
suppressed them,
and throttled my sobs,
you would spare me all this pain.
You might get embarrassed,
if you saw how often on my way to you I tumble,
how much hardship and humiliation I endure
Perhaps . . .
Perhaps . . .
Perhaps . . .
My biggest mistake, I came to know,
is that I forgot all routes that didn't lead to you.
I blocked my entire heart for you,
since childhood,
I signed you a blank check,
where you wrote down
my childhood,
my friends,
acquaintances,
my poems,
and all my days.
Now let's make a deal.
I have no energy left.
My remaining days can hardly accommodate any more wounds.
I have consumed all stocks of patience and tolerance.
I have spared nothing for the days to come,
because I thought you were my last destination.
I disbanded all my boats
and severed the wings of my heart.
I can't take it anymore,
so give me back my stock.
Your parting is still an open wound,
on my dignity's forehead.
Let's make a deal now.

It barely matters to you,
whether we stayed together or parted,
whether we exchanged false laughter,
or I alone cried.
I have left behind my loved ones,
deserted my hometown,
and joined you.
I have deserted everyone,
the streets, the whole world.
What have you done to keep us together?
What have I got in return?
I publicly put out my soul to you;
have you felt an urge to do so,
even between you and you?
Let's sign an exit deal now,
put out all your terms,
I will meet them all but one.
Whether you say it or not,
I am already gone.

A Frosted Cry

RUGAIA WARRAG

This morning the streets were covered in snow as usual.
The white clad was vast enough to kill
all warmth-producing cells in the weather's body.
Trapped in the cold of an interminable road
and the abyss of a seemingly perpetual exile,
I was attacked by a strong craving,
for a drop of my homeland's nectar,
and a gnawing urge for running away.
I slowed down my steps to hear myself wailing:
"*Wooooob! Wooooob!*
Woe on me, folks!
Woe on me!
I'm sinking in the snow!"
There I stood, waiting for some response,
but no one answered my distress call.
No neighbor jumped over the fence wall
to my rescue,
no relative to take me in their warm embrace,
my hands once again sought refuge in the warmth of my pockets.
And just before it frosted over, a teardrop said:
What a grave loss you've endured,
stranger.

A Tribute to Winter

RUGAIA WARRAG

Yesterday at 5:00 p.m.
in a dull, sad street
winter overtook me.
I saw a dream.
A tiny room,
in a house,
hidden in the hearts of thousands homes.
the light on and we are two lovers;
The light off and we are two lovers,
drinking tea from the same glass,
wrapped in the same blanket,
and warming our bodies
with the song we both love most.
In the comfort of that dream,
returning home at night
feels like coming home,
with a trophy in your school bag.
Bites of the severe cold wind
feel like friendly banter.
Winter's long nights cease to be
a storeroom of boredom—
And we cease to be anything but
man and woman.

The Spider's Text

Millennium Messages to Life

RUGAIA WARRAG

Translated by Mayada Ibrahim

(1)

> Forgive my question, O life
> And please don't get mad at me:
> Have you gone crazy?
> Can't you see I deserve much more rest time
> than you are providing me?
> So that I shouldn't waste away.

(2)

> Let me say it bluntly:
> Both you and I know
> that my perception of a relationship
> has little in common
> with those heavy burdens
> you continue to pile on me.

(3)

> You have showered everyone
> except me,
> with gifts of colored candy,
> but where is my tiny pack?
> I love them pink
> supple
> no chunks of dust in it.
> Please send some to my address:
> Sudan
> A five-year-old
> Brown-skinned girl.

(4)

You know how kindhearted I am
but that shouldn't mean people can do me harm
whenever they feel like it.
I need your help, life,
lend me some of your constraints
so I shouldn't shower my kindness
on those who don't deserve it!

(5)

I work away for hours
lending a hand in good faith to those who need it.
Yet, the results are below expectations!
Are you the one who marks my final exam papers?

(6)

I have been through tough times;
and I turned to a close friend for help,
but he gave me the cold shoulder.
Were you watching as he pretended to be dead?
Why didn't you warn him that you would give him a real death if he
    continued this farce?
But no. No. I beg you not to.
Forget about this complaint!

(7)

For reasons beyond me,
some people feel angry at me,
although I hate to offend anyone.
From your vast experience, are you able to tell
if they have a genuine reason to feel so?
Would you do me a favor telling them on my behalf
that it's their problem, not mine.

(8)

    You have incredible ability to invade my cells with amazing ease.
    You are so simple,
    So scaring.

(9)

    I've been let down many times
    during your course, O life.
    I can't tell how terrible it felt.
    As I told you, I hate to complain.

(10)

    I am not scared of you
    because I am part of you,
    And you are part of me,
    Yet I can't stop wondering
    how I will feel when we part!

(11)

    I hate to hurt others' emotions,
    Can I count on your help to see to it I am treated on equal terms?

(12)

    Will you one day help us probe the inner recesses of our souls?
    Or will that deep secret remain a perpetual source of pain
    for your sons and daughters?

(13)

    I know you despise selfishness.
    I can tell from the way you allocated the stock of breaths and heartbeats
    with unmatched fairness.
    Yet for some odd reason
    it seems you didn't pass this attribute down to your children.
    You didn't raise them up properly, I dare say.

Some of your sons wouldn't hesitate to snatch a bite off the teeth of their
    hungry brothers,
Some of your daughters wouldn't mind breaking each other's hearts,
Why shouldn't you raise your children properly, mother life?

(14)

Over the course of our union,
you immersed my heart in sorrows and deprivation,
My heart is now as clean and pure as an infant's.
Anything else you want to do to it?

(15)

Let us agree on a code,
a little secret code,
that you can send me,
the moment it crosses my mind to betray a dream.

(16)

On some rare occasions,
and because of you,
I had to treat a sister or son of yours roughly.
To be honest, I was acting in self-defense.
What is the point of putting me through difficult tests
when you know all the right answers?

(17)

You might have shown more leniency with me,
had I been less honest with you.
Don't take me wrong. I have no plans to betray my principles.
I'm a bit upset tonight. That's all.

(18)

Let me ask you:
Why do you put rough guys in the way of good women?

Is this your way of training your daughters?
I must say this is the worst training I have ever heard of.
You could have at least put only a few of them to such "training"
and let the rest learn from their experiences.
But the number of great women tied to bad guys is too vast.
This was not necessary, in my calculation.

(19)

Everyone is being put to test by someone else.
The child is tested by parents over homework.
The parents are tested by the child over his food needs.
Our next-door neighbor tests our tolerance of noise and bad manners.
We test our ability to maintain self-restraint and morale.
Writing tests our tolerance of pain and insomnia.
We, in turn, test its tolerance to stay with us to the end.
Our old home furniture tests our ability to live with its wretchedness.
We test its ability to withstand our heavy weights.
Our homeland tests our ability to stay away.
We test our expectations and memories.
Tests. Tests. Tests!
But who tests you, O life?

(20)

Our fears are always overestimated.
Each time I come to this conclusion
only after spending tremendous time and energy.
Next time please alert me with a signal,
like drawing out your tongue and tucking it back quickly.
I think I will understand;
I might even laugh at my fears

(21)

You do endow us with gifts, big and small:
Good health.

Money.
Loved ones around.
I'm not saying you should provide us with those gifts under guarantee,
with fixed expiry dates.
All I'm asking is you shouldn't go to the extreme in giving and taking.
I remember cases where some of my acquaintance lost their minds
    because of you!

(22)

Can I share my concerns with you at the end of each day?
And empty my heart into your big ears and open heart
without bringing myself to account?
Just to vent out my complaints. And you understand,
even when I can't express myself properly.

(23)

I hate loud voices.
What is the wisdom behind encountering them everywhere, my dear life?

(24)

And backbiting
Yes, backbiting.
You can see for yourself how many victims it has every single day.
Would you do something to address this, please?

(25)

Each year brings along numerous events.
These are turning into a source of irritation rather than entertainment.
I have no plans to celebrate anything this year.

(26)

I believe I am loving and devoted,
yet I am still lonely,
I don't understand!

(27)

One more favor from you, please:
I want you to help me wipe off all the smoke and dust clouding my
   mirror.
I look forward to seeing my channels of communication with others
   becoming pure, transparent, and pleasant.

(28)

It occurs to me sometimes,
behind your back,
that I am an incredibly unfortunate woman.

(29)

Disappointment
Grief
Crushed dreams
I have had enough of this vicious cluster of soul vitality depressants
Enough of them
I swear.

(30)

Give us more fun.
We need a break from a choking pile of tedious duties.

(31)

One can be as huge as an elephant.
yet with incessant buzzing a tiny mosquito can give a hard time to his
   super ears!
I expect your explanation of this grand mess.

(32)

Poverty is indeed our common enemy.
If we failed to conquer it,
please throw some caustic powder on its eyes.

(33)

I hope you wouldn't mind the question:
What do you mean by those weird incidents you keep weaving
    around me?
Are you a life or a spider?

(34)

Next time,
I repeat: next time,
send in my way a true soul mate.
Bring him close enough to my eyes so I shouldn't miss him.
Then just leave us alone.
Please make some genuine effort. Don't leave it to coincidence.
I don't mean to be a nagger,
but tell me: did you put this important request in writing on your
    priority list?
Or just toss it into your memory?
I would rather have it in writing.
Your memory is okay.
but I can't count on it on such vital matters.
Forgive my insistence, O life.
Just one last time before I leave:
Did you enter my request on the top priority list?
Please don't get mad at me,
but I haven't received a reply!
Any update on my request?

(35)

About the so-called limits—
The flag you so often raise on my face:
Let me be frank with you.
I have already started to tear it down.
Just wanted to let you know!

(36)

You are generally generous.
I will do my best to be generous as well.

(37)

From now on,
the moment I become aware of its existence,
I will exhale all the poisonous air you, perhaps inadvertently, pass into
    my lungs.

(38)

My self-conceit and naivety
sometimes tempt me to throw you out the window
after tearing you down like aluminum foil.
But when I remember we are destined to part at some point any way,
I dismiss that foolish thought
because it can deduct seconds from my credit with you
Even a single second, as you know, is a precious part of our mutual existence.

(39)

Why don't you call off all those rivalries among your sons and daughters?
Why don't you just give each one their deserved share?
This is no difficult task for one like you

(40)

I can't thank you enough
for the miracles you endow me with every now and then.
I love your miracles.
I always wait in anticipation for their coming.
I receive them cheerfully,
breaking the news to everyone.
What about a fresh one now,
after all the stupid events of the past months?

(41)

Is there a definite time when you will call off,
once and for all, all those curses and successive disasters?
Or will they continue to come and go freely?
How do you feel when they hit me?
Or rather;
why do you let it happen in the first place?

(42)

Do you feel the relationships between your sons and daughters are at their best?
Do you have better tricks you want to put to play
to address the issue of coexistence?

(43)

You know I have to be left to myself sometimes.
Please help me do that.
Remember, I didn't ask you to make loneliness my destiny!

(44)

I already feel sorry about my previous messages
when I said you didn't give me what I deserved
and other messages that reek of discontent.
Please forgive me for that.
Here you are, calling me hesitant
or even weak and inconsistent,
but I won't get angry with you.
I was just very candid with you
as candid as a woman like me should be with a life like you!

(45)

Those who cause us pain during your course are truly bad people,
They will continue to be so.
Although their painful blows yield a good deal of wisdom sometimes,
I do hope you will spare some time to address this evil tendency.

(46)

Wait a minute!
Have I ever said I wanted to "live" so seriously?
In which of your baggy pockets are you hiding my favorite toys,
my giggles,
my running around, dancing, sleeping.
There must be some fault in the way you allocated seriousness amongst us.
This lack of accuracy on your part has had its toll on me.
I want to see the matter fixed for my remaining credit with you.
And if it occurred to you to reward me with colorful bands of free time,
as compensation for my past forbearance and stressful time,
you will be amazed with the results.
You might have to cover your eyes with both hands
lest they be dazzled by millions of fascinating diamonds
glittering from the depth of my depths!

(47)

I am not begging you.
I will yell in your face; in all your corners,
if you ever give me that feeling again.
Stop giving me my rightful dues
as if you are tossing them over the wall.

(48)

You have taken my wedding ring.
Bring it back!

(49)

You have a strong power
but I have a strong sense of freedom.
Shouldn't we strike some deal
so no one of us should seek to stifle the other?

All Alone

KHALID HASSAN OTHMAN

A water jug, a cat, and a walking stick between us,
the lonely old woman tells me her story:
On my heart's grounds
so many brown-skinned children play
kicking around a ball made of old socks.
They play—(a smile)—in a lousy way
kicking off dust.
There on my heart's grounds:
soft dust
Gravels. Stones
Pits . . . and . . .
ashes.
The ball jumps about in my heart's airspace
nearly landing, like a gray bird, on a rooftop.
They never tire of playing.
Their chests heaving up and down on my chest.
Playing ceaselessly
at noon
in winter
they play
till sunset.
Clad in my heart's dust
their clothes lose their cleanliness
and acquire beautiful dirts.
I can't understand their jargon.
Loud voices.
Rough play.
My heart's net shakes so often.
There is a *zeer*[1]
offering passersby cold, sweet water.

The water owner is a woman whose grave is happy and soft.
Then. . . .
carrying its dark lantern,
night spreads its vast cloak,
wipes out dimensions,
wipes out the soft water.
My heart's night
wipes out the little ones.

Under Abundant Shades

NAJLAA OSMAN ELTOM

For some vague reason,
I still remember her face:
the tea-seller,
a teenager,
boiling the heavenly water of the Nile,
in her fresh mint,
and with her thin hand,
mixing milk and sugar.
O little girl!
Sweating out patience,
under the ruthless sun;
you are the carnation of this dark, rotten street,
packed with men
prudently chasing your defiant dress
and in the comfort of their abundant shades
grumbling about the heat.

Tuesday's Dilemma

I can no longer perform your name;
the audience is a flower drowned in your silence.
No worries, though
it'll all come to a halt.
I'll depart,
empty-handed, except for a manuscript
I snatched from the lips of my sweetheart.
Unveil has never been one of your names.
Calling you out is an act of deviance.
Your presence in my soul
is my sole territory.
You own it as much as a lavender lost between kisses owns the kisses.
O lovers,
learn my love codes,
learn the ones that give you not joy but terror,
sneak in and check out my humble place,
but don't feel ashamed of my sighs,
Watch me choke in my fears,
Pray then and pray again
for a similar haven.
Our dance,
our cruel dance.
My steps are hasty,
Maps born from my tears,
Roads from my sky.
My destination?
Why ask me? Can't you see it dancing in my pursuers?

An Acacia Bush in Labor

NAJLAA OSMAN ELTOM

I can't see you in my dreams,
but when I trace the burning thread slithering from my lungs,
all through your injurious prophecies,
I come face to face with deity.
Your face has no trace in my lineage,
you recoil upon your own truth:
a protrusion of solitude.
Somehow love comes to my rescue;
on the fifth sunrise,
flooded with coincidences yet using the pigeon ring as a pretense,
I call upon your forgotten abodes,
seeking not love but oblivion.
Blossoms are weighing heavily on my heart,
no wonder my dreams perish as fast.
I bury them under motherhood's staircase.
I'm now tied—hungry and faithless—to the cross of the glamorous mission,
planting birds on your anxiety-decorated uniform shirt.
How to reach one in limbo?
After a thousand years of emaciation
I destroy you
in a labyrinth you can't count on a moon guarded by your own lungs.
I sit before the sea of life,
the enemy is in,
enemy is me,
we sit shoulder to shoulder
munching screws of time and watching fear:
an acacia bush in rapid labor, running from one portrait to another.

The Fall of Angels

MAMOUN ELTILIB

Not a single year will pass without seeing one of the angels fall
not a single sorrow, without your images being under the mercy of the crowd.
Not a single brutality removed from the century's plate
until it is reinforced by your words.
The blade is dried with a towel pregnant with our sun, and all our moons
a towel used to dry your blood
for a peace flag to fly.
against every window that set a bird free is an executed angel.
Beneath every river
are shoals of fishes escaping nets
only to die on the up tide.
The depth of the well is an abode
for unborn insects and snakes,
but only rats are born there.
That is where we fetch our drinking water.
From that window,
we watch them falling, our angles
Which window? The one opening inward?
Where collective skulls crave for a boil with life in the same corpse?
The window overlooks rivers that are still there
and will continue to be!
And so will the seas.
The oceans will not shrink
and friction can only yield fire.
Sounds will remain there,
winds will blow,
and storms will continue to be born forever.

Wrapped in Grief

BOI JOHN AWANG

Wrapped in grief,
my heart reduced to a wreck,
my soul to a vague memory of a life,
I invite pythons and scorpions to me,
"I am your feast. My blood is your toast."
Wrapped in grief,
I invite darkness to my eyes,
and the snow to my skin.
O grief octopus,
be nice to me. Crush my bones.
Sprinkle the ashes of hope over me.
Order the torrent to wash away my image,
and the clouds to drift away my grave.
Wrapped in grief,
O thunderstorm: come die inside me.
Envelope me, O flash of lightning, like a cocoon.
Add me, O flying clouds, to the spectrum.
Wrapped in grief,
thirsty,
like a roaming dervish,
in the midst of nowhere.

Skies

1

I wish my killer would sleep on my body!
and the birds seeking refuge in music would hug me.

2

The sky is afloat on your face.
Everything is paying allegiance to you.
Even the sand grains I spread on your way
can't wait to embrace your steps.
I'm desperate for a glimpse of hope from you.
Sorry to wake you up at this late cycle of love.

3

(Two birds sipping the cold breeze, teaching the trees how to dance, how
    to give birth to eternal lovers dangling on Pio Yikwan Street.)
"Take left, sweetheart. Before winter hits us."
(The crazy wind blowing from seas of passion are setting your braids
    ablaze, scorching my fingers.)
"Give me a kiss, sweetheart, before spring passes us by," two passion-
    soaked eyes say.
I say: "Your eyes have taken everything in their embrace. Your lips are
    silent utterances.
Every night I sleep on your eyelids. Alone there I spend a sleepless night."
"Pour me a shot, sweetheart. I need to sober up."
"I haven't had enough shots from your eyes."

4

My soul is perplexed
fraught with perils—and poetry.
Take in my body, darling—into you.

Transform me into words
Roses
A sky besieged by tragedy.
Transform me into you
so I can fly.

5

I'm still waiting for you
at the sunset where you left me
Sleepless
Composing poetry
Reflecting
Waiting for the return of our past moments
at Palace Avenue.
Your late arrival
exciting and packed with surprises
like how it feels when you see a friend from afar
but he vanishes to thin air.
I vanish in my waiting.

6

If I can sing,
the mountains would shout: here's a lover for you.
I would crush air and gravel
would wake up Abu Daoud[1] from his eternal slumber.
Together we would sit and drink,
and pour golden nights onto the ears of the universe.
I would leave my body
crucified on al-Hallaj's cross.
The flow of your tears would be enough to irrigate bushes forever.
The deeper I drown in my annihilation
the more tempted you grow in hugging me.
Can you see?
Yes!

Through your ears' imaginative power
you can see things that no poet ever saw,
things that never hit a lover's heart.
If I can sing,
the trees would let out its eternally concealed truth
I would tear out the veils on your brains
so you could see the path to the Lord in plain sight.

7

Tears spill down from the window
Your face spills down on nature
Nature spills down on my palms
My palms blossom.
I drink your face.
How many eyes touched your eye
Putting off the cosmic lantern lit by Sayed Abdel Aziz"² one Sudanese night.

8

Do you have a heart playing violin, sweetheart?
Do you have a sky like the one I have?
How dearly do you miss me?
I miss you to death!
Do you have a body that can see the world?
How can you look in the mirror when you are its eye?
Can you see me?
I am inflicted with the moon, with your eyelashes, with sleepless
     loneliness.
Say everything, sweetheart,
before I spill down the plains and deserts
before the moon sips off my insight!

9

Who will serve me a shot?
Yes, friends.

A glass of that golden music
A glass of the lethal life
A glass stolen from skies yet to be created.
Who?
Then, "Long live love."

On the Bank of River Sobat

NYLAWO AYUL

On the bank of River Sobat
a detached umbilical cord is buried
and five words I kept in my pocket
isolation and wisdom
light and virtue
and the shade of a vague pain on thick lips
My lips shooting at a hollow point
My mouth trying to shed off the burden of words
and the dagger.
Among the burnt grass I went searching
for the old pastures
for a fallen mango fruit
for a wave with a golden light
pointing to the direction of eternity
to the south
The abode of the papaya
in the warm land
The grazing haven for cattle
and the sticky clay bond—
But what I saw was a bird
carrying the blue silence toward the Nile
The water's sadness was pink
The decomposed fish
The sum of daily carnage
The war mark on the body of the south
And yeah—the tall stalks of grass
They die when elephants choose them as battleground
and the tall folks cherishing the dream
of a south simple and beautiful
but they die in war.

An Amulet for the Mango Tree

I have to pass through the town dogs,
the morning music,
and gunfire,
to inscribe this poem on the trunk of the mango tree
as a memoir to bluff a rainy day.
Weather is merely a coaxed smile,
sliding through a hole in a baffled sky,
oozing obscurity,
like a conjurer's song in a cold January night.
But this poem must be a lily,
or a live calendar in an ancient song,
carved on the secret entrance to eternal darkness;
or a woman wearing her summer slippers
firmly shaking her head and saying:
You are alive, sweetheart
The shade of your shoes has a vague resemblance to a gun,
that transformed into Prometheus.
Women know how death can be pleasant,
so they prefer to leave windows open,
and the mango tree smiling,
and the night, or this fleeting feeling
that resembles existential questions interwoven between thunders
and the storm outside the window
or the elaborate agony of watching the sky falling apart
when the men go to war
because women know that soldiers are the best lovers;
they know that soldiers put lace on the trigger's shade
and write their poems on the woman's body with the scent of air
but my poem inscribed on the trunk of the mango tree

could not dare promise an imminent arrival of dawn
or a lovely death in the warmth of your palms
because her glittering letters have drowned
in the deep blue of the powder smell.

INTRODUCTION

1. Qurayshis and Tamims are prominent Arab tribes.

MY BELOVED AAZZA

"Aazza" is Sudan's most popular patriotic song. It was composed, put to music, and sung by Khalil Farah (1894–1932), a nationalist figure and an activist for independence. Aazza is a common female name in Sudan that means pride and dignity; it is used allegorically here as a patriotic symbol. Almost a century now since it was composed, "Aazza" is still highly celebrated and sung by young generations of Sudanese, as well as musicians from Russia, France, Korea, Ethiopia, and others.

DIG NO GRAVE FOR ME

An elegy for Abdel Khaliq Mahjoub (1927–71), former secretary-general of the Sudanese Communist Party. Mahjoub was a prominent politician and a highly influential figure in international communist forums and devoted his life to building an indigenous formula for Marxism in Sudan. He was executed in July 1971, in the aftermath of an aborted coup attempt against President Gaafar Nimeiri's regime.

YAAQUT AL-ARSH

Yaaqut al-Arsh (died 1287) was a renowned Sufi figure in Alexandria, Egypt, where el-Fayturi spent a good part of his youth.

AN AFRO-ASIAN SONG

This poem was written in celebration of the birth in 1961 of the Non-Aligned Movement, which was a middle course for states in the developing world between the Western and Eastern Blocs during the Cold War.

1. Om Sabir is an old Egyptian woman who, during British rule, used to supply Egyptian resistance fighters with ammunition that she kept hidden in her dress.
2. An antithesis of a famous poem by prominent Arab poet Ahmed Shawqi lamenting the division of ranks of Arab countries (the Orient). Shawqi's wording was: "We, as people from the Orient, are united in sorrow and grief."
3. This refers to the Joudeh massacre in 1956 when approximately two hundred peasants protesting for their rights were arrested at gunpoint and held in a tiny, poorly ventilated building used as a store for agricultural pesticides, where they died of suffocation.
4. The Suez Canal, referring to President Gamal Abdel Nasser's bold decision to nationalize the strategic waterway.

A DRIB OF YOUR NECTAR

1. *Khilassiyah* is one of mixed racial descent.

SONGS FOR OCTOBER

The title reflects the 21st of October 1964 Revolution that toppled the military rule of General Ibrahim Abboud (1958–1964) and restored democracy in the country.

MONOLOGUE

This poem was composed in 1989, while the poet was being detained at Cooper (Kober) Prison, Khartoum North, Sudan.

THE SILENT ROSE

1. Zarqaa of Yamama refers to a legend of a keen-sighted girl who lived in the Arabian Peninsula. Zarqaa was blessed with eyes that were not only beautiful and blue but could see long distances away. So she served as a fully fledged detection system, warning her tribe of any invasion. Legend had it that in one particular invasion attempt, the approaching army covered themselves in tree branches to avoid her radar. When Zarqaa warned her tribe that an army of

trees was approaching, they dismissed her warning as nonsense, until the enemy attacked them.

NURA AND THE TIME-TESTED DREAM

1. A tambur is a locally made musica instrument.
2. The *donka*, is the food preparing area.
3. A *fekki* is a religious person.
4. A *baseer* is a traditional healer.

ALL ALONE

1. A *zeer* is a clay pot cooler that does not use electricity.

SKIES

1. Abu Daoud is a famous Sudanese singer.
2. Sayed Abdel Aziz is a famous Sudanese poet whose love poems were put to masterpiece songs and are still popular among the Sudanese of all generations.

REFERENCES

Abbakar, el-Nur Osman. 1967, "Lastu Arabiyyan walakin" [I am not an Arab, but . . .], Khartoum, *Al-Sahafa Daily*, September 19.

———. 1970. *Sahw al Kalimat al-Mansiyyah* [Awakening of Forgotten Words]. Khartoum: University of Khartoum Press.

Abdul-Hai, Muhammed. 1973. *Al-Awdah ela Sinnar* [Sinnar: A Homecoming]. Translated by Mustapha Adam. Khartoum: University of Khartoum Press.

Abdel Rahman, Jayli, and Taj el-Sir el-Hassan. 1991. *Qasayed min al-Sudan* [Poems from Sudan]. Beirut: Dar al-Jeel.

Abu Zikra, Abdel Raheem. 1973. *al-Raheel fil Layl* [Parting at Night]. Khartoum: University of Khartoum Publishing House.

Ahmed, Khalid Hussain. 1995. *Mawso'aat al Babtain lil Shi'r al-Arabi* [Al Babtain Arab Poetry Encyclopedia]. Riyadh: Abdul Aziz Saud Al Babtain Poetry Foundation

Badawi, Abdo. 1981. *Al-Shi'r fe al-Sudan* [Poetry in Sudan]. Kuwait: Aalam al-Ma'arifa Series, National Council for Culture, Art, and Letters.

Elgizouli, Kamal. 2004. *Omdurman Ta'tee fe Qitar al-Thaminah* [Omdurman Comes on the 8 o'clock Train]. Cairo: Dar al-Oloum Publishing House.

———. 2017. "Al Thuqb fe Saqf al Bayt: Jadal al Hawiyyah wal Wihda fe Hiwar Mutakhayyal bayn al Shai'rayn Salah Ahmed Ibrahim wa Sirr Anai Kelueljang" [The Hole in the House's Roof: The Dialectic of Identity and Unity in a Fictional Encounter between Two Sudanese Poets]. Khartoum: Hurriyat Online Magazine.

El-Khatim, Abdel Goddous. 2012. *Muraja'at fil Thaqfa al-Sudaniyyah* [Reflections on Sudanese Culture]. Omdurman: Abdel Karim Mirghani Cultural Centre.

El-Makk, Ali. 1980. *Mukhtarat min al-Adab al-Sudani* [Selections from Sudanese Literature]. Khartoum: University of Khartoum Publishing House.

Fat'h el-Rahman, Elyas, and Hayder Ibrahim Ali. 1996. *Jayli Abdel Rahman: Sha'ir al Waqt fe Siyaqin Aakhar* [Jayli Abdel Rahman: A Poet of Time in a Different Context]. Cairo: Sudanese Studies Center.

Hussain, Jabir. 2014. "Abu Zikra: Howa la Yureed al Mawt Raghman Anhu," Al Baieed online literary magazine, http://www.albaeed.com/.

Ibrahim, Abdullahi Ali. 1996. "Al-Afroarabiyyah aw Tahaluf al-Haribeen" [Afro-Arabism or the Alliance of the Escapists], in *al-Thaqafa wal Demogratiyah fil Sudan* [Culture and Democracy in Sudan]. Cairo: Dar al Ameen.

Ibrahim, Mohammed el-Makki. 1969. *Ummati* [My Nation]. Beirut: Dar Al-Awda.

———. 1972. *Ba'dhul Raheeqi Ana wal Burtuqalatu Ante* [I Am a Drib of Your Nectar; You Are the Orange]. Khartoum: University of Khartoum Press.

Ibrahim, Salah Ahmed. 2000. *Nahnu wal Radaa* [Death and Us]. Khartoum: Madarek Publishing House.

———. 1959. *Ghabat al-Ababnous* [The Ebony Forest]. Beirut: Al Hayat Bookshop Publishing House.

———. 1965. *Ghadbat al Hababay* [The Rage of Hababay]. Beirut: Dar el-Thaqafa.

———. 1967. "Bal Nahnu Arabul Arab" [Verily, We Are the Arabs at Their Best]. Khartoum: *Al-Sahafa Daily*, September 19, 1967.

Jamma', Idris. [1984]. *Lahazatun Baqiyah* [Eternal Moments]. Khartoum: Dar al-Fikr Publishing House.

Munif, Musa. 1985. *Mohammed el-Fayturi: Sha'ir al Hiss wal Wataniyyah wal Hubb* [Mohammed el-Fayturi, a Poet of Sensations, Patriotism, and Love]. Beirut: Dra al-Fikr al-Libnani.

Shammat, Lemya. 2018. "A Review of Abdel Goddous el-Khatim's *Reflections on Sudanese Culture,* 2012." ArabLit online literary magazine.

CONTRIBUTORS

Khalil Farah (1894–1932) was a nationalist figure and an activist for independence. Born in Saai Island, northern Sudan, he grew up in Omdurman and studied mechanical engineering at Gordon Memorial College. Farah was an ardent fighter for independence. He was a member of both the Sudanese Union Society and the White Flag Society and took part in the 1924 revolt against British rule. His powerful poems were instrumental in stoking anti-colonial sentiments.

Muhammad el-Mahdi el-Magzoub (1919–1982) was born in el-Damar, northern Sudan, to a renowned Sufi family. He graduated from the School of Accountancy at Gordon Memorial College (now the University of Khartoum). El-Magzoub was a transgenerational poet who tackled virtually all forms of poetry, from the classical to *taf'ila* all the way to prose poetry. He is widely regarded as the godfather of the Jungle and the Desert group, which espoused a third way from the Arabism and Africanism in Sudanese culture. El-Magzoub left behind ten collections of poetry.

Idris Jamma' (1922–1980) graduated from Dar al-Uloum (now Cairo University) in 1951. He obtained a diploma in education from the Teachers' Training Institute, Sudan, in 1952 and worked as teacher in different parts of the Sudan. His posthumous poetry collection, *Lahazat baqiyah* (Eternal Moments) was highly acclaimed by critics and poetry enthusiasts.

Mohammed el-Fayturi (1930–2015) was a poet and playwright who was born in Sudan to an Egyptian mother and a Sudanese father of Libyan origin. He published scores of poetry collections, including *The Songs of Africa* (1956), *Lover from Africa* (1964), *Remember me Africa* (1965), *A Roaming Dervish's Stanza* (1969), *Smile for the Horses to Pass* (1975), among others.

Jayli Abdel Rahman (1931–1990) was born in Saai Island in northern Sudan. At the age of nine, he migrated to Egypt to join his father. He studied at al-Azhar and later in Moscow where he pursued post-graduate studies in arts. Jayli is regarded as one of the pioneers of the foot poem in the Arab world, which heralded a major departure from the ages-long traditional poetry. He is also credited with translating a large volume of Russian poetry into Arabic. He left behind two published and three unpublished collections.

Mohyiddin Faris (1936–2008) was born in Argo, northern Sudan, and migrated to Egypt as a child, where he had his primary, intermediate, and high school education in Alexandria and his university education in Cairo. Faris is regarded as one of the pioneers of Socialist Realism in Arabic poetry, with seven collections to his name.

Taj el-Sir el-Hassan (1935–2013), a poet and university lecturer, was born in Artoli, northern Sudan. He graduated from al-Azhar in 1960 and from Maxim Gorki Literature Institute in 1966. His published poetry collections include *Poems from Sudan* (co-authored with Jayli Abdel Rahman, 1965), *A Green Heart* (1968), *Two Poems for Palestine* (1991), *Poetry in the Time of Oppression*, among others.

El-Nur Osman Abbaker (1938–2009) was born in Kasala, eastern Sudan. He graduated from the Faculty of Arts, University of Khartoum in 1962 and earned a diploma to teach English as a Second Language from Leeds University in 1970. He worked as teacher of English language and literature in Sudanese high schools and as translator and editor of al-Doha Magazine (1980–1986). His published anthologies of poetry include *The Awakening of the Forgotten Words*, *Songs for the Grass and the Flower*, and *The River is Unlike Clouds*.

Mohammed el-Makki Ibrahim (b. 1939) is a poet, writer, book critic, and political analyst. He earned his BA in law from the University of Khartoum and his MA in political science from the Sorbonne. A career diplomat, he served as Sudan's ambassador to Pakistan, Czechoslovakia, and Congo, as well as a diplomat in Paris,

Prague, Saudi Arabia, and Sudan's mission to the United Nations in New York. He was a political analyst with the Embassy of Qatar in Washington DC and an assistant professor at the Defense Language Institute. He has numerous publications, including four books of verse, a collection of satirical essays, and hundreds of articles published in the Arab media.

Mustapha Sanad (1939–2008) was a prolific poet, with six collections: *The Old Sea* (1971), *Glimpses of the Old Face* (1978), *The Return of the Sea Penguin* (1988), *Papers from the Time of Crisis* (1990), *Inscriptions on the Memory of Fear* (1990), and *Our House on the Sea* (1993).

Abdel Raheem Abu Zikra (1943–1989), was born in Tangasi al-Soug, northern Sudan. He studied Russian language and literature in Moscow and obtained a PhD in linguistics from the Russian Academy of Sciences. He translated scores of poems by prominent Russian poets. His sole poetry collection, *al-Raheel fil Layl* (Departing at Night), was published in 1973.

Ali Abdel Qayyoum (1943–1998) was a poet, playwright, and film director. He studied arts at the Ministry of Khartoum and cinema in Poland. He taught cinema and applied criticism at Khartoum Higher Institute for Music and Drama. He was one of the founders of the University Theater Group at the University of Khartoum and a founder of the Apademak Group. He left behind one published anthology, *al-Khayl wal Hawajiz* (The Horses and the Barricades), one play, and one film.

Muhammad Abdul-Hai (1944–1989) was a prominent Sudanese poet and literary figure. He studied English literature at the University of Khartoum and later earned a master's degree from Leeds University and a PhD from Oxford. He was associate professor at the University of Khartoum and director-general at the Department of Culture, Sudan. He published five volumes of poetry, including his seminal work, *The Return to Sinnar*.

Kamal Elgizouli (b. 1947) is a lawyer, poet, literary critic, journalist, and human rights activist. He studied law and international relations at Kiev State University in the former Soviet Union. Kamal's publications include three major collections of poetry, including the critically acclaimed *Omdurman Comes on the Eight O'clock*

Train. He has published six other books and hundreds of articles on diverse topics ranging from culture and politics, literature and literary criticism, to issues of peace, democracy, civil war, and human rights. Elgizouli is a founding member of the Sudanese Writers' Union and served as its secretary-general until 2007. He is an honorary member of PEN International.

Aalim Abbas Mohammed Nur (b. 1948) was born in al-Fasher, western Sudan. He graduated from Omdurman Islamic University in 1972. His published anthologies include *The Rhythms of the Raging Time* and *Trees of the Grand Questions*.

Mahjoub Sharif (1948–2014) was a poet, teacher, and activist, who became known in Sudan and other Arabic-speaking countries for his colloquial poetry and his public engagement, both committed to furthering the causes of democracy, freedom, and national identity. His poetry was put to music by eminent musicians, such as Mohammed Wardi, but also led to repeated political imprisonment under different Sudanese governments.

Mahgoub Kbalo (b. 1949) is a poet and literary critic who graduated from Cairo University at Khartoum. He has one published poetry collection, *Sikirtair al-Hugool* (Secretary of Meadows); one play, *Muhakamat alNafar al-Thalith* (The Grand Child Trial); and scores of literary essays and critiques. He is a member of the Sudanese Writers Union.

Fidaili Jamma' (b. 1951) is a poet and writer, born in al-Mujlad, Kurdufan. He studied at Khor Tagat High School and the Faculty of Arts, University of Khartoum. He has a number of published collections of poems.

Abdulqadir Alkutayabi (b. 1954) is a poet and writer. He was born in and grew up in Omdurman. He has published four collections of poetry and one of essays.

Mohammed el-Hassan Salim Himmaid (1956–2012) was one of the most popular poets in Sudan. His folk poetry is highly celebrated by different generations as it echoes the frustration of the poor and downtrodden. He published seven collections of poetry, all written in colloquial Sudanese Arabic. He died in a tragic traffic accident near his native village of Nuri, in what seemed like a reenactment of the tragedy of "Uncle Abdur Raheem," the protagonist of this epic poem. The poem went viral when put to music and sung by the great composer-singer Mustafa Sidahmed, who met a no less tragic end, dying in exile after a long struggle with renal failure complications.

Hashim Siddig (b. 1957) is a poet, playwright, critic, and journalist. He earned a B A in criticism from the Music and Theatre Higher Institute in Khartoum in 1974 and did further studies at the School of Acting in Essex, United Kingdom. He wrote more than ten poetry collections and scores of plays for radio, T V, and theater.

Azhari Mohammed Ali (b. 1954) is a poet and civil activist, born in the second half of the 1950s. He writes in dialects and has two published collections: *Waddaha*, and *Toobaa lil Ghurabaa* (The Blissful Strangers).

Al-Saddig al-Raddi (b. 1969) grew up in Omdurman where he lived until forced into exile in 2012. From 2006 to 2012, he was the cultural editor of *Al-Sudani* newspaper until he was sacked from his position for political reasons. Saddig's first poetry collection *Songs of Solitude* was published in 1996 (second edition, 1999). He has also published *The Sultan's Labyrinth* (1996) and *The Far Reaches of the Screen* (1999, 2000).

Rawda el-Haj (b. 1969) is a prolific poet, with five collections to her name. Her poetry is celebrated across the Arab world. She has won several literary awards.

Rugaia Warrag (b. 1965) studied philosophy at Cairo University (Khartoum branch) and sociology and gender studies at Brock University, Canada. A journalist and human rights activist, she now lives in Canada where she works as interpreter.

Khalid Hassan Othman (b. 1968) has two published poetry collections: *Tamatheel* (Statues) and *Gharghaa fil Miyah aljameela* (Drowned in the Lovely Water). He works as translator in the UAE.

Najlaa Osman Eltom (b. 1975) is a Sudanese writer and translator who has been active in the literary scene in Sudan since 2000. Her first poetry collection came out in 2007. As a female writer in a literary tradition dominated by male figures,

Najlaa had to deal with the complex questions of voice, individuality, taboos, image, and performance of a female writer. Thus, individuality, fragmented and contaminated female body, and violence are recurrent themes in her work. Najlaa has lived in Sweden since 2012.

Mamoun Eltilib (b. 1982) is a poet, writer, journalist, and cultural activist. He served on the executive committee of the Sudanese Writers Union from 2006 to 2007 and from 2011 to 2013. He is the founder of several cultural initiatives, such as Mafroosh, which is focused on promoting the exchange and recirculation of books. He has one poetry collection forthcoming.

Boi John Awang (b. 1983) is a poet and novelist from Sudan. He belongs to the young generation of South Sudanese novelists and poets who write in Arabic.

Hatim Al Kinani (b. 1982) is a poet and journalist. He works as staff editor for *Al-Baeed* online magazine and *Al-Hadatha* magazine. He has two published poetry collections: *Al-Yanabei Taghsilu Awazaraha bi Yadayk* (Springs are washing their sins with your hands) (Khartoum Publishing House, 2013) and *Wardat Adam* (Adam's Rose) (Al Musawwarat Publishing House, 2016). He has many articles published in local and regional newspapers and magazines.

Nylawo Ayul (b. 1986) was born in Malakal, Upper Nile province (now part of South Sudan). She studied psychology at the University of South Carolina at Chapel Hill and now lives in Canada. She has one published collection, *Qarabeen Nekang* (Nekang's Immolations), and a second one under publication.

Logotherapy
Mukoma Wa Ngugi

When the Wanderers Come Home
Patricia Jabbeh Wesley

*Seven New Generation African
Poets: A Chapbook Box Set*
Edited by Kwame Dawes
and Chris Abani
(Slapering Hol)

*Eight New-Generation African
Poets: A Chapbook Box Set*
Edited by Kwame Dawes
and Chris Abani
(Akashic Books)

*New-Generation African Poets:
A Chapbook Box Set (Tatu)*
Edited by Kwame Dawes
and Chris Abani
(Akashic Books)

*New-Generation African Poets:
A Chapbook Box Set (Nne)*
Edited by Kwame Dawes
and Chris Abani
(Akashic Books)

*New-Generation African Poets:
A Chapbook Box Set (Tano)*
Edited by Kwame Dawes
and Chris Abani
(Akashic Books)

To order or obtain more information on these or other University of
Nebraska Press titles, visit nebraskapress.unl.edu. For more information
about the African Poetry Book Series, visit africanpoetrybf.unl.edu.

Lightning Source UK Ltd.
Milton Keynes UK
UKHW041136160220
358787UK00011B/51